THE
ORGANIST

THE
ORGANIST

Fugues, Fatherhood,
and a Fragile Mind

MARK ABLEY

 University of Regina Press

Printed and bound in Canada at Friesens. The text of this book is printed on 100% post-consumer recycled paper with earth-friendly vegetable-based inks.

Cover design: Duncan Campbell, University of Regina Press
Text design: John van der Woude, JVDW Designs
Copy editor: Ryan Perks
Proofreader: Kristine Douaud
Cover art: "Modern Organ" by Alex Potemkin / iStockphoto
Interior images: page 2—Harry Abley as a child, c. 1922. Courtesy of the author;
    page 160—Harry Abley at the Organ, c. 1976. Originally published in the
    Saskatoon StarPhoenix. Every reasonable effort was made to acquire permission.

Library and Archives Canada Cataloguing in Publication

Abley, Mark, 1955-, author
    The organist : discovering my father in music and melancholy / Mark Abley.

Issued in print and electronic formats.
ISBN 978-0-88977-581-7 (hardcover).—ISBN 978-0-88977-582-4 (PDF).
—ISBN 978-0-88977-583-1 (HTML)

    1. Abley, Harry, 1917-1994. 2. Organists—Canada—Biography.
3. Depressed persons—Canada—Biography. 4. Abley, Mark, 1955-. I. Title.

ML416.A152A15 2019   786.5092   C2018-906081-6
C2018-906082-4

10 9 8 7 6 5 4 3 2 1

University of Regina Press, University of Regina
Regina, Saskatchewan, Canada, S4S 0A2
tel: (306) 585-4758 fax: (306) 585-4699
web: www.uofrpress.ca

We acknowledge the support of the Canada Council for the Arts for our publishing program. We acknowledge the financial support of the Government of Canada. / Nous reconnaissons l'appui financier du gouvernement du Canada. This publication was made possible with support from Creative Saskatchewan's Book Publishing Production Grant Program.

Henry Thomas Abley
1917–1994

Mary Muriel Collins Abley
1916–2012

Oh the rising of the sun
And the running of the deer,
The playing of the merry organ,
Sweet singing in the choir.
—"The Holly and the Ivy," traditional English carol

'Tis strange that death should sing.
I am the cygnet to this pale faint swan
Who chants a doleful hymn to his own death,
And from the organ-pipe of frailty sings
His soul and body to their lasting rest.
—William Shakespeare, *King John*

This book is nothing if it is not a genuine slice of life. There was an extraordinary mixture of comedy and tragedy in the situation which is here described, and those who are affected by the pathos of it will not need to have it explained to them that the comedy was superficial and the tragedy essential.
—Edmund Gosse, *Father and Son*

PROLOGUE

Some years after his death, my father appeared in my sleep. It was the night of his birthday, the twenty-fourth of March.

My mother was with me in the dream. As it began, she and I agreed the time had come to bury his ashes. We stood side by side in a small stone church. The organ was a few steps from the door. But soon we found ourselves outside the church, near a path that ran through a graveyard. It was evening. Light snow was falling.

My father's ashes had been packed inside a long tube, the sort that tennis balls are sold in. After I dug a hole in the ground, my mother and I opened the tube and poured out the ashes. They lay there, a pale powder in the dark soil. I felt obliged to speak, but uncertain whether to attempt a prayer or a eulogy. "Rest in peace" seemed the obvious phrase, and a wrong one. Eventually I found a few words to say.

When I had finished speaking, I didn't want to leave the ashes exposed, and I began searching for the wooden fragments of a gravestone—within the contours of the dream, this made perfect sense. I walked back to the church and stood by its door. A choir was practising inside.

The choir emerged from the building in a procession, and one of the singers suggested I look for the fragments at the far end of the cemetery. I followed her advice but when I saw the pieces, they seemed to be just scrap wood. Even so, I picked them up and carried them back to the grave. I was surprised to find them fitting neatly in place, like the blocks of a jigsaw puzzle, above my father's ashes.

Then I took up the spade again, and shovelled dirt on top. I was alone: the choir had vanished, and my mother was nowhere in view. Evening had dissolved into night.

I looked up and saw my father standing above me. Had time swept me back into childhood? Or was I now the one in the grave? He was wearing a black cassock and a white surplice, as though he had been playing the organ. It was very dark, yet light must have been coming from somewhere, for I could see him clearly.

I said nothing. My task was to listen.

At last he spoke. His tone was stern. Looking down at me, my father said, "Did you know I was more than you made of me?"

PART I

FANTASIA

1 A small hotel on the south coast of England, set back a few streets from the sea. My father had come to Bournemouth for sandcastle holidays as a boy, and now, at the end of an exhausting vacation with his wife and son, he may have wanted to recall or recreate some of the happier experiences of his early life. My mother didn't care for the town. I was fifteen. It was the last time my parents would take me on holiday with them. In a few weeks, I would enter my last year of high school. I was slipping away from their grasp. Or should have been.

A small hotel, constructed in the Victorian era as a home for a man of means. The property had later been converted to serve tourists. Bournemouth lingers in my mind as a blur of rock candy, congested sand, and a long walk through a fern-strewn valley beyond the shops and the brick houses. Walks with my parents were always problematic. My father liked to stride ahead, stopping only to admire the most extravagant of views. But my mother preferred to hang back, alert for any unusual tree or wild-flower, keen to listen to birdsong in the wood. At such times they annoyed each other. I was an only child. I vacillated between the two of them.

The hotel was old and modest enough that it had no private bathrooms. A deep, chipped bathtub dominated a cream-painted room at one end of the hall. The toilet stood in a minuscule chamber beside. Every morning we would descend a wide flight of stairs to consume one of those "English breakfasts"—fried bacon, fried egg, fried tomato, fried potato, fried bread—that seem the quintessence of fat. My mother, who had not eaten red meat since childhood, would leave her bacon on the far side of the plate. We lubricated the toast with cups of steaming tea. It had been less than nine years since we settled in Canada, and my parents still needed tea in the morning. So did I. It would take another Saskatchewan winter before I acquired the taste for coffee.

This was our last breakfast of the trip. Where had we been in the previous few weeks? My memories are fragments, strands of displacement and desire: an evening listening to early Cat Stevens albums with a girl in Warwick; the stink of cheap cigarettes in a Woolworth's café; the sight of lapwings and curlews high over the moors near my parents' birthplace in the Welsh borderlands; the sexually provocative graffiti on a wall at Edinburgh Zoo. But

I thought of myself as a Canadian. I had a few friends at home. I wanted to go back—I even felt a tinge of excitement at the prospect of the long plane trip.

We would have to board a coach from Bournemouth to Heathrow Airport. My mother, efficient as always, had packed the suitcases and organized the hand luggage. Everything was ready for our departure.

But where had he gone?

My father was in the lavatory down the corridor from my parents' room. I don't know if he and my mother had traded harsh words. They sometimes did. But they stayed together regardless, bound by need and duty and drawing on some deep, secluded pool of love. We had to leave this seaside town in less than an hour. Why was he taking so long?

My mother went to ask, and obtained no answer. My father was not an inarticulate man—he could hold forth in long, bitter monologues if he chose. But he had what my mother called "an artistic temperament," along with a talent for remaining silent. On that summer morning, silence was all that my mother received.

Her first reaction, I assume, was anger: "Don't be ridiculous! We've got a plane to catch. It's time to come out now."

Silence. Immobility.

She knocked on the door of my bedroom. Was I reading the morning's *Guardian* or *The Lord of the Rings*? My mother's skirt and blouse were as tidy as always, her lipstick applied with precision, yet she looked flustered, her manner strange, as though the fabric of her carefully woven life were at risk of unravelling. "You try. He just refuses to unlock the door. He's being impossible."

I walked down the corridor, my running shoes light against its dark red carpet, and tested the handle of the lavatory door.

"Dad, it's me. It's Mark. Please come out of there. We've got to get to the airport. We can't stay in Bournemouth forever."

Silence.

"We'll be late for the bus! Come on, Dad. I want to go home."

My first home had been a semi-detached house on a busy road in Coventry, an industrial city in the English Midlands. My second home was a bungalow in Sault Ste. Marie, a few blocks away from the river dividing northern Ontario and the Upper Peninsula of Michigan. Most emigrants leave their native country once and for all—but not my parents. My third home was the ground-floor flat of a big house back in Coventry, where I started school. But soon we set off again, this time to the town of Lethbridge, in southern Alberta. For several months my parents rented a small apartment above a Chinese-Canadian corner store. By the time I turned seven, I had lived in six buildings.

We moved on to Saskatoon a few years later. Saskatoon was where I belonged now; it had to be. In the throes of high school, I couldn't allow myself the luxury of divided loyalties. My father's concept of home was more nuanced, more complex.

Silence. My mother joined me. She spoke in her most gentle voice.

"Bunny, listen. Do listen to me. You know we have to be on our way. Bunny, the coach will be leaving soon."

Years earlier, they had abandoned the use of each other's given name in favour of private nicknames. My mother was never "Mary" on my father's lips, but always "Woggo" or "Polly Wig" or simply "Mum." Likewise, he had ceased to be "Harry" inside the family home. He called himself "Nubbo" or "Nub," the reverse of "Bun," short for "Bunny Hunch," a play on "Honey Bunch"—a term that had, after the birth of his only child, been jettisoned.

"Are you all right in there, Bunny? Do unlock the door."

Was he sitting on the toilet, was he standing up, were his trousers down, did he have a grip on the door, was his greying head in his hands? I didn't have the least idea. The grandfather clock at the end of the hall was ticking remorselessly away.

My turn. "Dad, please! Come out! This isn't funny anymore. I'm sorry if I upset you somehow, but we've got to leave!"

The world was spiralling into chaos again. This was always a danger of life in my home, life with my parents, but it was a special peril of holidays: they seemed to bring out all the latent tensions in the marriage. Driving east across the dry interior of Washington, three years earlier, my parents had argued so fiercely that they decided to seek a divorce. I slumped in the back seat of the blue Volkswagen Beetle, carsick, yearning for oblivion. By the time we made it back to Lethbridge, two motels later, some kind of reconciliation had occurred. I inferred this from the fact that my father failed to move out of our rented stucco bungalow, though nothing was said to me directly.

A summer before that, on the road from Salisbury to Winchester in southern England, my mother had so angered my father that he, the only driver in the family, stopped the rented car in what seemed, to an eleven-year-old boy, the sun-swept middle of nowhere. The battle lasted long enough for dozens of cars to speed by. It ended with my father spinning the vehicle around and driving back in the direction from which we'd come. We would not, after all, visit another of my mother's uncles. The uncle would, after all, die a year or two later. She would not, after all, forget. It would take her years to forgive.

Holidays were dangerous: I knew that. But this latest one had passed without more than a couple of my father's sudden, unpredictable blowups. Normally the mildest of men, he could explode into an aggressive rant or a burst of self-pity and vicious self-hatred that had the power to darken my entire world. I was familiar with that. But I had never known him to lock a door, remain dead silent, and refuse all pleas to venture out.

My mother's turn. "Bunny, don't be so selfish. I'm ashamed of you. I'm ashamed and upset. This is absurd—you know we have to catch that plane. It's not going to wait on the runway. We can't stay in Bournemouth any longer."

Silence. I remember an old man stepping down the hall, gazing curiously at a black-haired, middle-aged woman and a teenaged boy reasoning with a locked door. The old man's head jerked back and forth. Humiliation: the wash of it across my face and ears. My hot, reddening ears. My heartbeat pounding against my temples like the English Channel's onrushing tide.

"Look, Dad, this isn't fair. I hate it when you act like this. What do you want us to do?"

Silence. Below my black-rimmed glasses, tears were trickling down my face. But I wasn't going to let my father know. He was stubborn. He had his pride; I had my pride too.

"Bunny, how could you? How *could* you?"

At last my mother walked back along the corridor to their shared bedroom. Or she went down to the reception desk on the ground floor in search of help. However it happened, I was left alone in front of a door. On the other side of it, I knew, I must have had a father.

I tried again.

"Dad, I just want you to know, your music means a lot to me." I swallowed hard. "I'm proud of you. I'm really glad you're an artist…"

At the time, I wasn't proud of him; I was embarrassed and furious. But a brilliant inspiration isn't always the whole truth.

I'm really glad you're an artist. When he heard me say those words—words I had never spoken before—my father unlocked the lavatory door and stepped into the hall. His tie was neatly fastened; his parting looked immaculate as ever, the combed-over hair just about hiding his bald spot. He gave no sign of remorse or anxiety. I was a curly-haired wreck.

I don't recall a hug, still less a kiss, but we made it onto the Heathrow coach and we caught the plane home.

2 Each of us walks the world in camouflage. Each of us can be a mystery to ourselves, never mind other people. I'm sure I baffled my father, just as he baffled me. He died more than two decades ago, and as the natural, necessary process of forgetting takes hold, any picture I draw of him becomes an exercise in self-portraiture. There are some things I can't forget. But there's much I struggle to remember. The work compels me to blend my own features with his.

Harry Abley had a range of identities. He was a son, a husband, a father, a devoted football fan, a migraine sufferer; a proud Canadian and a lifelong Englishman; a close friend of almost no one. At various moments, he worked as a medical records clerk for City Hospital in Saskatoon, a demonstrator of electronic organs at the Eaton's department store in Sault Ste. Marie, and an assistant to the North American zone controller in the export branch of Standard Motor Company in Coventry. (That was in the

1950s, when Britain still shipped cars across the Atlantic.) He had no affection for any of these jobs. He did them for the money.

Above all, my father was a musician. He played, he conducted, he taught; he accompanied; he composed. When I was a boy, he would sometimes appear at the dining table with a pencil behind his right ear and an abstracted look in his hazel-green eyes. After a few bites of food and a cursory exchange of words, he would excuse himself, return to the piano—the central item of furniture in each of his many homes—and play, over and over, some musical phrase. Just a few bars at a time, with tiny variations: a chord with D flat, a chord without D flat; a staccato phrase, a legato phrase; a five-note melody, a six-note melody…Listening to him, short-sighted as I was, I thought about how my optometrist would keep toying with the refractor's glassy settings to arrive at a correct prescription. When a melody or chord had been fixed to my father's satisfaction, and he had scribbled it down on the back of a used envelope or the previous Sunday's church bulletin, he would resume his meal. My mother could be a stickler for proper manners and polite behaviour. But she tolerated these whims without complaint, knowing they were anything but whims. When my father was composing music—for choir, organ, solo voice or piano, and occasionally for other instruments too—he was happy, or something approaching it. Those were the good times, the times when nobody had to worry about his state of mind.

The piano took pride of place in his living room. He would never be at home without one. But the instrument of his life was always a walk, a bus ride, or a drive away: the pipe organ. My father had been learning the piano for four years when, as a boy of twelve, he started organ lessons. He fell in love; he remained in love. A small man with the habits of an introvert and the remnants of a boyhood stammer, he could sit down at the organ bench and fill a cavernous church with as much sound as an entire orchestra. In the Middle Ages the organ had been nicknamed the "King of Instruments," and my father relished the phrase. He was a prince while performing. The feeling of power this gave him must have been exhilarating. It compensated, no doubt, for much else.

As a teenager, Sunday after Sunday, I heard him play and watched him conduct. Pipe organs are like no other musical instrument: listeners in an audience or congregation rarely see the performer at work. The organist sits at a semi-enclosed console—a term that refers to the keyboards, pedals, and draw-knobs or "stops" on either side of the musician—usually hidden behind a pillar or screen, or placed high up in a gallery at the back of a church. There my father would use both hands to play the keyboards and both feet to play the pedalboard. On rare occasions he might push in a stop with an elbow. The mental discipline required to play a difficult piece for organ is matched only by the physical coordination. The resulting waves of sound emerge from metal or wooden pipes attached to a wall, some distance from the console. Yet to a casual listener in the pews, organ music is born independent of the performer; or so it seems.

When my father was conducting a choir, he might climb down from the organ bench and stand in the central aisle. Now the visible focus of attention, he would make no sound himself; instead he would use his hands and arms to shape the sounds produced by other people. In style, his conducting was precise and undemonstrative. He disliked conductors who flung their arms around, and he admired Sir Thomas Beecham, the founder of the Royal Philharmonic Orchestra in London, for his ability to direct musicians with a single finger. The robes my father wore in church lent him a certain stature; they emphasized the critical role he believed music should hold in worship.

His profession sent the calendar topsy-turvy. He held choir practices and gave private music lessons on weeknights and Saturdays; the office hours that other people kept were a time for him to practise the organ, learn new pieces, and plan the music for services to come. Sunday was the height of his week, its morning worship the climax and justification of the six preceding days. And to my father, what justified a service was its music. At lunch afterwards, he would seldom mention the sermon—while the priest or minister was holding forth in the pulpit, my father liked to shut his eyes and allow his mind to wander—but he welcomed comments about the prelude, the hymns, the psalm, the anthem, the improvisations, the postlude.

Music showed him a way to God. I suppose it would be an exaggeration to say that for him, music *was* God; perhaps, though, his God was a heavenly version of Johann Sebastian Bach, a divine artist able to create structures of such transparent beauty and intricate complexity that the cosmos would ring out in harmony. In each of their homes my mother placed a crucifix on the living room wall, and my father hung a portrait of Bach on the wall above his desk. Music ruled his life.

It did not rule mine, and therefore his was a life I could not fully enter. I never took an organ lesson; maybe he was waiting for me to ask, maybe I was waiting for him. More likely, he needed to maintain a private space away from the demands of his family, just as I needed to create an imaginative world in which my parents would not be dominant. An organ, any organ, no matter how shrill its tone or limited its range, would give him the space he craved. Not every organ held stops that allowed my father to speak with both the *voix celeste* and the *vox humana*. Yet he was a master at coaxing beauty out of unlikely vessels, making even the weakest instrument sound sweet or strong. To his wife and child, the language he lived and breathed was a foreign tongue: the language of a distant nation. The language of organists.

I look in his big scrapbooks, where he meticulously recorded the details, great and small, of his musical life. They tell me that on June 17, 1943, he was "permitted to play, by recommendation, the magnificent Concert Organ at Alexandra Palace, one of the largest organs in Great Britain." By whose recommendation, I want to know? What kind of music did he play? Alexandra Palace, perched atop a hill with a commanding view over North London, was the site where during the Second World War the Royal Air Force used a BBC transmittal system to jam the navigation signals of German bombers. Did anyone from the RAF or the BBC come to hear him perform? The scrapbook answers none of these questions. Instead my father recorded the names of the four keyboards ("manuals" in organ parlance), and the quantity of thumb pistons for each of them, and the noteworthy fact that the organ boasted "3 Swell Pedals, which may be coupled to any of the manuals, at the desire of the performer." What else did the performer desire?

His was a checkered career, I suppose, one that never quite lived up to its extraordinary early promise. The class-bound nature of English society, the long interruption of the war years, the hard struggle to keep Britain's economy afloat in the postwar decade: all these are reasons why. But there are other reasons too, ones that involve my father's temperament and character. He believed in his own skill as an organist. He was also convinced that he had been hard done by—he felt he had not received his due. This combination of beliefs did not make for peace of mind. At times my father seemed to be equally gifted at music and resentment.

Even so, there was much to be proud of. In old age, if he had been the sort of man to look back in pleasure, he could have done so with ease. He did not lack for admirers. But the applause, the admiration, the appreciation were like scraps of gauze barely hiding the wounds below. Have I ever met a person more profoundly alone? He brushed away his accomplishments like rainwater. After his death, I found in his wallet a quote from Henry David Thoreau, cut out long ago from a newspaper and taped onto a fragment of cardboard: "I was not born to be forced. I will breathe after my own fashion.…If a plant cannot live according to its own nature, it dies; and so a man."

Beside the cardboard was a tattered *Peanuts* cartoon, clipped from the *Saskatoon Star-Phoenix* in the years of my father's greatest professional success. Peppermint Patty and Charlie Brown are leaning against a wall, peering over it. "I need to talk to someone who knows what it's like to feel a fool," Patty says. "Someone who knows what it's like to be humiliated. Someone who's been disgraced, beaten and degraded…someone who's been there." In the final image of the strip, Charlie Brown says nothing. He just opens his arms wide.

My father carried that cartoon around for more than a decade. At some point he took a pencil and, in big capital letters, added a trilingual note: ME! MOI! MIR!

3 "If you bring forth what is within you, it will save you. If you do not bring forth what is within you, it will destroy you."

So Jesus declares in the Gnostic Gospel of Thomas. I have kept silent far too long, and I don't suppose it will save me now to tell the story of my father. But I fear it may destroy me if I don't.

It's not entirely my father's tale, of course. That's a saga only he could have told, and he shied away from the task. My mother's hard-won habit of looking cheerful, looking on the bright side, looking out for saving graces, may explain some of his reticence; she was a woman of profound religious faith, and blessed by hope. Outwardly her own life contained fewer achievements than my father's, but she remembered much of it with gratitude and was willing to speak freely. At bedtime, when I was a child, she would tell me stories about her childhood in rural Wales and her years as a schoolteacher in Warwickshire. Once, in a coal-mining village near Coventry, the fathers and brothers of her pupils dared to invite her down the pit; she dared to accept. I fastened on these stories. I needed them.

Not to speak about his life was my father's choice. The past was a battlefield full of unexplained skirmishes, and he had no desire to inform his son about the explosions that deformed the landscape. We remained silent, and the silence corroded us both. I knew none of my grandparents, and grew up without the least idea of what my father's parents had looked like. He never talked about his beloved mother, who died soon after his fifteenth birthday; half a century later, it would have hurt too deeply. He never talked about his father, either. That may have been a form of revenge, or simply an urge to forget.

This is, then, also a story about myself—the story of an anxious boy who grew up to be an anxious man. Like my father, I showed great promise as a child. A few weeks after his mother's death, he came first among his age group in an organ competition held across the United Kingdom: an astonishing feat for a shy, grieving, tongue-tied boy from an obscure little town on the Welsh-English border he would come to dismiss as "the last place on Earth." As for me, I was skipped ahead two grades in school and won a succession of medals, prizes, and cheques. None of them began to show me what it might be like to feel whole.

Happiness has always come to me in moments, often the product of solitude and nature, sometimes of poetry and alcohol. Since I became a husband and a father, I've discovered with surprise that family life can also bring joy. But even now, at the far end of middle age, I struggle to understand what it means to be a man. Even as I'm praised for my gentleness, I'm told there is some kind of absence about me. If so, the absence has much to do with my father.

I've managed to forget a lot. I stand in suspicious awe of memoir writers who show an effortless capacity to recall the sights, sounds, and smells of their childhood. For me, I suppose, forgetfulness became a necessity. Was it only in the year when I was badly bullied, or was it over a much longer period, that I chanted under my breath, *I-want-to-die-I-want-to-die-I-want-to-die…*? Eventually it struck me that one day I would get my wish. I clogged my brain with useless information—by the age of twelve, I knew the name of every capital city in the world and could identify each country's flag—so as to forget, or avoid facing, other knowledge.

Even so, some things lodged in me, clung onto me. I carried them around for years, clutching them like private totems: talismans of grief. Every now and then, I would take one out to polish, saying to myself, under my breath, "If only they knew…" I married an extraordinary woman whom I met at Oxford, and there were certain memories

I kept from her. One thing I had absorbed from my father was the art of concealing the past. If you take the risk of speaking out, I felt, you leave yourself vulnerable—you display your wounds. You advertise your scars. You put yourself at somebody else's mercy.

Four years after our wedding, Annie and I having moved to Montreal, we were invited to dinner in the apartment of a couple of poets. They were spending eight months in the city, one of them as a writer-in-residence at Concordia University, but for the previous few years, they had lived in Saskatoon. They knew of my lingering reputation there—the boy wonder of the English Department—and they were unimpressed. Patrick challenged, confronted, disturbed me. He was, I felt, unimaginably *free*. That night I drank so much red wine that, from the impacted depths of an anger and shame I had always been too scared to probe, I drew out a story:

"It was a Saturday evening in Lethbridge, a few years before we moved to Saskatoon. Dad was organist and choirmaster of First Baptist Church. In the morning he would have to play for a service. And my parents had a terrible argument.

"I don't know what it was about—I must have been nine or ten at the time. Before adolescence, anyway. I was trying to watch *Hockey Night in Canada*. Snow was falling. And when my mum had got the better of the argument—she was the one skilled with words, the one who'd thought about becoming a journalist—my dad left the house. He went to the closet for his overcoat. He wasn't shouting anymore, he seemed deadly calm. He just put on his coat and scarf, his gloves and overshoes, and walked out the front door.

"Mum and I stood at the window and watched him go. He had his wallet in his jacket pocket—for all we knew, he could have been leaving for good. We had no idea where he was going. He didn't take the car, he just marched away into the night. I remember the streetlight catching his footprints in the snow. He didn't look back once. My mother was terrified that he wouldn't show up at church the next day.

"We stayed by the window for a few minutes. And when it was clear that he wasn't coming back, my mother turned to me. She already had her hand around my shoulder. She looked at me and said, 'You're more of a man now than he'll ever be.'"

Mother and Son
(Lethbridge, 1964)

You are the voice in the kitchen singing;
I am the smell of new-washed linen
in a summer bedroom with the window open

before drowsiness tucks me in and silence falls.
You are the ladies' book-club member;
I am the furtive reader of *Anatomy
of a Murder.* You are the steady
towel beside the bathtub, the avid
hands that clasp a gold report card; I am
the dripping body, I am the
reported gold. You are the heavy-lidded eyes
battling tears at Mr. Abley's
new absurdity or old tirade;
I am the spiteful giggler; together
we conspire. You are
the warm front; Mr. Abley is
the cold front; I am the weather's edge.
You are the crucifix above a bookshelf;
I am the word made flesh. You
are all memory; I am
all forgetting, all struggling
to forget. You are the sleepless
presence waiting; I am an absence
waited on, moist fear withdrawing into
new-washed lemon sheets;
I overhear your lovesong by the counter
and my small heart thumps assent.

4 My father was a little man. Not a tiny man: he claimed to stand five foot eight, although I suspect he may have exaggerated by an inch. Even in the Canadian West there were littler men, I knew. But children are unfair—*I* was unfair. After the first nomadic months in Lethbridge my parents rented a bungalow: a living room, a kitchen, a pair of bedrooms, one cramped bathroom, and a mostly unfinished basement. The walls were coated in a coarse stucco the colour of lead. My father drove a Volkswagen Beetle, a much smaller vehicle than most Alberta men owned in what was still the heyday of tail-finned, Detroit-made cars. Having been pushed ahead in school, I was always among the smallest boys in my class. This wasn't a great challenge to begin with; then everyone else arrived at puberty and I did not.

I was always conscious of my father's musical talents, yet I wanted him to cast more of a shadow in the world. Ross, my best friend in elementary school, also had a

British mother—a war bride, swept off her feet by Ross's father. He was a quiet man too, someone who worked in an agricultural research station, but during the Second World War he had served as an officer in the Royal Canadian Air Force, taking part in bombing raids over Germany. My father, so far as I knew, had done nothing more glamorous in the war than drive trucks by night through a rain-soaked, blacked-out England. What danger could there be in that? Ross's father wasn't much taller than my own, but when he strode into the rumpus room I could see my friend's pride.

The church I attended on Sunday mornings was also small. My father played the organ and directed the choirs at one of Lethbridge's grander churches, but my mother didn't like the prospect of my being overexposed to Baptist doctrine. We lived near Henderson Lake, on the south side of town. Across the tracks, on the working-class north side, stood a white-painted Anglo-Catholic church named St. Mary the Virgin. And for years my mother and I caught a bus or cadged a ride to a Sunday service she always called "Mass." The priest there wasn't just a "Reverend," he was a "Father," and a bulkier one than my own. But I encountered him only once a week, at the altar.

The decision to remove me from First Baptist Sunday school, where I'd spent a few innocent months, may have coloured the way I saw my parents as a child. Inside the house, my father always deferred to my mother. Domestic chores and responsibilities were hers alone. In church I could have seen him in his element, admired by many, respected by all. But for most of our time in Lethbridge, I rarely set foot in First Baptist.

There were exceptions, of course. On one snowy December night I was allowed to stay up long after my bedtime to watch my father lead a complete performance of *Messiah*. It brought together three choirs, which he had rehearsed for many weeks. Handel scored *Messiah* for a small orchestra with organ (his favourite instrument was shipped from London to Dublin for the premiere); in the Lethbridge version, all the orchestral parts were adapted for the organ. The King of Instruments, indeed. My father could have asked another musician to take over at the console, allowing him to concentrate on the choirs and the seven soloists; or he could have asked someone else to conduct, allowing him to focus on the organ. But he performed both tasks, playing the entire instrumental score while directing dozens of singers. *The people that walked in darkness have seen a great light*: the packed church, chilly at first, grew warmer and warmer. I sat beside my mother, awed and proud. *For unto us a child is born*: far away on the organ bench, my robed father was at work.

From time to time, he reviewed concerts for the *Lethbridge Herald*. Now that newspapers across the

English-speaking world have shrunk to anorexic proportions, and many of their editors would scoff at the idea of reviewing classical music, it's salutary to realize that in a Prairie town of 35,000 people, the local paper had both the space and the desire to run such reviews. In truth, my father didn't write them, although they appeared under his name. He went to the concerts and jotted down notes; then he came home and told my mother what he thought. She turned his ideas into publishable prose. The perceptions were his, but the final words were hers. Later they adopted the same pattern in writing program notes for the Saskatoon Symphony Orchestra. I could have looked on all this as a superb example of married teamwork, but, recognizing some of my mother's turns of phrase, I regarded it instead as proof of how my father would have been lost without her help.

Boys don't need their fathers to be heroic. Very few fathers in Lethbridge had flown in bombing missions against Nazi targets. Yet even if the men had done nothing to win the war, I imagine most of their sons looked up to them regardless. Had my father not been so prone to denigrating and belittling himself, I wouldn't have seen him as so small. He never talked about the physical and mental control that a big pipe organ demands, nor his encyclopedic knowledge of the organ repertoire. That would have been boasting, something to which my parents were allergic. "Self-praise is no recommendation," my mother often said. I wasn't encouraged to dwell on my own successes, merely to bask in her loving devotion.

Yet my father trod a fine line between humility and humiliation: at times he took a perverse satisfaction in being slighted. Any snub, no matter how trivial or off-hand, could affect his mood for days. "I like the Welsh," says a character in Bruce Chatwin's beautiful novel *On the Black Hill*, which is set in the border country my parents came from. "But they do seem to get so angry, later." My father dealt with grudges by nursing them tenderly and venting them bitterly.

On Lethbridge Sundays, he and I would go for long walks together while my mother was preparing dinner—although she would not eat lamb, beef, veal, or pork, she was happy to roast flesh for us. We often trudged around Henderson Lake, walking through the park and along the edge of a golf course before making our way home past a baseball diamond and along the city's broad, straight streets. I had no idea that the lake had been created from a swamp known as Slaughterhouse Slough. During those walks, my father would hold forth. I said little in reply. It was a chance, as my parents might put it, for him to let off steam.

He would tell me about the English football club he followed so avidly—Swindon Town, usually mired in the Third Division, sometimes at risk of dropping into the

Fourth. They had a long history of mediocrity, interrupted once by an alarming triumph in the League Cup. As a young man living in London, my father had occasionally bought a ticket to watch Arsenal, Tottenham, and other top clubs play, but he didn't care about those teams now. Swindon, the home of his mother's mother, was the footballing love of his life. The players wore red uniforms and were nicknamed the Robins—feisty and musical birds, though tiny by comparison with the Lions, Stags, Red Devils, and Wolves. Swindon was the perpetual underdog.

In the current era of online fandom, I can indulge my love of the Detroit Red Wings in the knowledge that thousands of other people across North America are even more ardent in their support than I am. If I can't recall offhand who the Red Wings picked in the sixth round of the last junior draft, it takes a few seconds to find the answer. But to my father, self-exiled in Western Canada long before the birth of the Internet, backing Swindon Town was a quixotic and lonely pursuit. He kept a pocket diary in which, game by game, year by year, he would record Swindon's results, the players who scored (if any), and the size of the crowd. The diary was a proof of allegiance and a means of keeping faith. In his later years it served two purposes, musical and sporting, so that "Wrote GIA Publications (Chicago) re my BAS mass" would be followed by "Newcastle 5, Swindon 0. 28,600."

On our walks I was constantly aware that my father maintained his English accent. I had ditched mine a few months after our arrival in Lethbridge, when I happened to be the only child in my Grade 3 class who could answer a question the teacher asked. I was sitting in the front row, a common fate for children whose surnames began with "A." "Aren't you ashamed," the teacher said to the other pupils, "that you don't know the answer but this little English boy does?" I felt thirty pairs of Canadian eyes boring into my neck.

England was where my father's tongue lay, and his heart. He would talk not only about Swindon Town but also about the English national teams in football and cricket. And by some leap of logic or imagination I could never follow, he went on to deplore the injustice of the capitalist system and rail against the power of millionaires and big corporations. Sometimes he would even find reasons to praise the Soviet Union. My mother reminded him occasionally that he had, out of loyalty to Winston Churchill, voted Conservative in the 1945 election that saw Britain elect a Labour government; my parents were engaged at the time, and she had voted Labour. Since then Britain had moved right and he had shifted left, far left. Respectable to the point of formality in his clothing, his manners, his job, he held some beliefs that were downright unrespectable.

The personal grievance that my father nursed against the United States dated back to the 1940s. Hitler's war had not made him anti-German; Dresden had been destroyed, Hamburg and Mainz all but obliterated, and no matter how great or small an event, he instinctively sided with the losers. He believed that Germans had paid their price, and he bore them no ill will. Loss had transformed them into underdogs. His resentment, instead, was aimed at the GIs who had swaggered through England as if they owned the place—"overpaid, oversexed, and over here," the saying went. I'm not sure if he knew the caustic rejoinder: that British soldiers were "underpaid, undersexed, and under Eisenhower."

The second word in that phrase is not the only one my father would have hated. As a boy, half-comprehending at best, I listened to long harangues about the uselessness of American soldiers and the superiority of Field Marshal Montgomery to General Eisenhower. Having no opinion, I kept quiet. When he was in a mood to talk, and not just about the war, my father seldom wanted to hear anyone else's views. His speeches bored me and sometimes unnerved me. But I listened, for I needed a father.

Today, when I try to recreate the exact words he used in his complaints and rants, I struggle. Stray words come back to me, random phrases, but what were the cadences he found to put them all together? "I've had it," he would say; the meaning of "it" was infinitely variable. "It" would "get on my nerves." Criticism would be met by "Stop getting at me!," the stress placed on the preposition. One of his favourite adjectives was "pifflin'," a reversal of "flippin'," itself a substitute for another f-word. Even when I was a boy, "pifflin'" struck me as oddly childish; it was not a term I ever used. On occasion my father would say his blood was boiling, a phrase that made me uneasy. But the line I associate the most with his rants was a simple one: "I ask you!" As with "I've had it," the emphasis lay on the middle word. My father turned "I ask you" into a statement of pure frustration; no question was implied, no answer sought. "The pifflin' minister was getting at me again this morning. It makes my blood boil. He wants me to play jazzed-up hymns! I ask you."

If I ever inquired about his own boyhood, my father would clam up, and I knew already that his silence was more disturbing than his words. Silence could mean he was brooding about the griefs and failures of his life. His silence was a locked room, and I didn't have a key. My father carried an enormous weight of grievance on his shoulders, and the only way he could lift it even slightly— apart from music—was by transferring the blame onto some remote and powerful foe. There was a God in his world, but very little justice in it. In Lethbridge we must have made an odd sight: a small, grey-haired man with a ruddy complexion, striding past a baseball diamond without glancing at the game, and holding forth about history, politics, and English football to a speechless boy in glasses.

The shadow that my father cast was one of misery and frustration. Or so it appeared to me. Whatever he had aspired to as a child, whatever he had dreamed of, it was not a suburban park in a wind-beaten town near the Rocky Mountains. Even as he marched around Henderson Lake with his anxious son, he had immortal longings. At some point in his life he typed out a few lines from *Gitanjali*, a work by the great Bengali poet Rabindranath Tagore. He always kept this sheet, no matter what else he discarded. "Gitanjali" means "song offerings," and this was one of my father's:

> The song that I came to sing remains unsung to this
> day.
> I have spent my days in stringing and unstringing my
> instrument.
> The time has not come true, the words have not been
> rightly set; only there is the agony of wishing in
> my heart.

5 Trust me. I'm telling you the honest truth. I'm not
making anything up.

Don't trust me. "What writers do," Kazuo Ishig-
uro once said, "is stroke the wound."

6 I am looking at a children's book and wondering why it used to terrify me. *The Child of the Temple* was published by Ladybird Books in 1952—"one of the most wonderful stories in the Old Testament," the dust jacket says, "beloved by children everywhere. In this book, Miss Lucy Diamond tells the story of the boy Samuel and Eli, the priest, in very simple and homely words all can understand; and Mr. Kenneth Inns has charmingly captured the Eastern atmosphere in his colourful illustrations."

I have my suspicions about Mr. Inns. When Samuel can be no more than five years old, he appears to be wearing bright red lipstick and a sleeveless dress. As he grows older—eleven, say—his hair develops an elegant wave and he sports a patterned skirt with little bells dangling down to his knees. Even at night, when he wakes to hear a strange voice calling, he keeps his lipstick on. It could be the colour reproduction, I suppose. Except for the skirt and bells.

But it was the story, not the pictures, that worked its way under my skin. When the tale begins, Elkanah and Hannah have no children. Elkanah—a shy and somewhat remote man—doesn't mind the absence of a child. "Yet Hannah was sad! Sometimes she sat and cried for hours and refused to eat." A strong, black-haired, apparently middle-aged woman with a distinct resemblance to my mother (courtesy of Mr. Inns), she steals away from Elkanah to pray alone in the temple at Shiloh. "Give me a little son! If only you will give me a little boy of my own, I will give him back to you, to serve the Lord Jehovah all the days of his life."

She goes home and gets her wish: "By and by she had a little son." No mention of Elkanah playing any part in the process—I guess we have Miss Diamond to thank for that. Certain types of simple and homely words were evidently beyond her. "Baby Samuel was the most precious thing in all that beautiful house—and how tenderly his Mother watched over and cared for him!"

Yet as soon as Baby Samuel can dress and feed himself, his parents get rid of him. They haul him off to Shiloh and hand him over to the old priest. Eli is taken aback. He recovers quickly, though, and welcomes Samuel into the temple. An illustration shows Hannah and Elkanah riding off into the sunset while Samuel waves goodbye and Eli grips the boy's neck. "Such a little boy to be left all alone with strangers without his father and mother!" Samuel is compelled to be brave: he has become a child of the temple, a refugee in a house of God. With her son in holy exile, "Hannah was a happy woman now. She and Elkanah had other children, three sons and two daughters."

Then, one night, Samuel awakens in the shadowy temple and hears a voice calling. He jumps up and runs to the priest, but Eli is fast asleep. The voice is persistent. "Samuel!" it calls again. And again, and again. After the third mysterious summons, Eli tells the boy what to do. Instead of hurrying back to the old man, "little Samuel whispered, 'Speak, for your servant hears.'" The voice proves to be that of the Lord God. He informs Samuel that one day the boy will take Eli's place—that he, rather than one of Eli's own sons, is destined to fill the role of high priest.

As a small child, I took several confused messages from all this. One was that no matter how much my parents loved me, they might be scheming to hand me over to the Lord, possibly even in a skirt with bells. After all, my father earned his living by making music in a house of God, and my mother was the most faithful and knowledgeable Christian I knew, clergy included. The second implication was that if I had any faint hopes of obtaining a brother, I might have to accept this kind of sacrifice. Third, and most ominous of all, was that whenever I woke up in the night, I'd better stay quiet and listen hard. That rustling noise below my window might not be a stray cat in the flower bed or some poplar leaves swirling in a dry wind; it might be the voice of God, calling to me as I crouched beneath the blanket. Wasn't I, like Samuel, a special, longed-for, firstborn son? I was scared shitless.

I sensed already that my mother hoped I would enter the priesthood. She spoke to me fondly about celibate Anglo-Catholic priests she had known in England, one of whom had pledged his heart and soul to Our Lord while continuing to live at home with his mother. Even in my wretched innocence, even in my devotion to Mum, this did not seem an enticing future. As a teenager in Saskatoon I attended church every week, spending a few years as a server (Anglicans avoid the term "altar boy"), but it must have been clear to all—I hope so, anyway—that I had no vocation for the priesthood. Secondary ambitions seized hold of my mother: that I would join the diplomatic service or acquire a skein of degrees. Ambassador Abley, Professor Abley…Nobody on either side of my family had ever been to university. A step that seemed only natural to me was a major leap to my parents.

Or, if all else failed, I might become a writer. It was a Mark, after all, who had composed the earliest gospel.

What my father hoped for me was less clear. If he dreamed that I would follow him into the realm of music, he gave no indication. I was about eight when I began to study the piano. But I didn't learn this skill from my father. Instead, once a week, I went on an afterschool trek across Lethbridge to the basement studio of a gifted, chain-smoking pianist named Henry Waack. By a sort of barter system, Mr. Waack dispatched one of his six sons to take lessons from my father. Neither Dougie Waack nor I showed any sign of turning into Vladimir Horowitz. After a few years of this exchange, my family moved to Saskatoon. Without an immediate counterpart of Mr. Waack in the new city, I stopped having a weekly lesson and gave up the piano for good. The last thing in the world I wanted to be was like my father. Besides, I was in high school by then, and had other things to think about. I suspect this callow decision—this necessary, self-protective decision— hurt my father deeply. But he never expressed an opinion on the subject. Or if he did, I have managed to forget.

In my second-last year of high school, psychology reared its head. "Psychology" with a capital "P," that is: a half-year course, taught by the school's guidance counsellor. Was it joyless Freud, beginners' Skinner, youngsters' Jung? All I remember is that for three straight classes we explored the problems faced by only children. They had trouble making friends; they were egotistical and oversensitive; they hated sharing any of their belongings. They were, in general, spoiled rotten. My classmates and I had been born late in the baby boom, when parents were repeatedly fertile. All except mine, that is. I was the only only child in the class.

I told my mother. She was outraged. She was also upset that, according to Psychology, only children enjoyed but one advantage over their sibling-happy peers: financial. With fewer mouths to feed and fewer bodies to clothe, the parents of only children were supposed to have money to burn; their pampered darlings owned more toys and dressed more smartly than children with a brother or sister. This was, I felt, demonstrably wrong. In Canada my parents never owned a house, my father always drove a modest car, and at Christmas most of the other kids in school opened more expensive presents than I did. Perhaps, though, this error in the textbook was a blessing of sorts: it meant I could also laugh off the textbook disadvantages of my solitary condition, disadvantages that seemed, deep down, to hold more than a grain of truth. I was convinced we weren't as wealthy as most other families because I knew exactly what my father was paid for his work at St. John's Cathedral. Every month the *Star-Phoenix* would reveal the average income in the Canadian labour force, and my father made nowhere near that figure. As my vocabulary grew more sophisticated, I decided that my parents were trying to maintain a middle-class lifestyle on a working-class salary.

What I didn't realize was that in a yearly bout of civil disobedience, my father lied on his tax return. He was a freelancer, not just a salaried employee, and he never declared the income he earned from his private teaching. He must have thought of music as a non-taxable gift, or a spiritual entitlement. As far as I can tell, he cheated the government of Canada for more than twenty years. If anyone in the government ever caught on, they may have decided there was no point in pursuing a man with no significant assets except a skill at the pipe organ.

7 When my children were young, I bought a CD of Halloween noises to play as the trick-or-treaters ran up our driveway, bags in hand, asking for candy. Annie and I inserted a black lightbulb in the fixture over the door, laid plastic spiders' webs across the handle, and placed a life-sized bat in a window. The carved pumpkins were as jagged-toothed as I could make them. The final touch, I thought, would be banshee shrieks and wails emanating from the living room. Only when I played the CD did it dawn on me that these shrieks and wails would be accompanied by organ music. My father had died a few years earlier, and the beloved instrument of his life had been falling silent in my own.

As he well knew, the pipe organ has an odd, schizophrenic reputation. It's easy to have no opinion about the viola or the bassoon; it's harder to have no opinion about the organ. The noise it makes can be painfully loud—no other musical instrument, without an amplifier, emits so much sound. And in the realm of popular culture, the organ belongs to Dracula. In a low-budget horror movie from 1960, *World of the Vampires*, an aristocrat raises the undead by the scary music he conjures from a pipe organ made of human skulls and bones. He flees when he hears a cheerful tune, performed on the piano by the virtuous hero. *Sesame Street* has a purple-faced Muppet named Count von Count, doubtless a Transylvanian, who plays a pipe organ while counting up to the number of the day. The villain of Disney's *Beauty and the Beast: The Enchanted Christmas* is Maestro Forte, a pipe organ with an English accent; he schemes to prevent the Beast from falling in love with Belle. On a more grown-up level, the splendid overture in the movie version of Andrew Lloyd Webber's *Phantom of the Opera* begins with the sound of a full-voiced pipe organ, whose ferocious arpeggios and pedal melodies smash the quiet and introduce the themes of anger, frustration, and pain that afflict the tormented anti-hero.

"The organ," Alex Ross once wrote in the *New Yorker*, "is an enormous machine on which any idiot can make an impressive noise." Persuading it to make good music is a trickier proposition. The instrument has, Ross noted, "a diabolical appeal: one touch of a button can unleash mayhem." Diabolical: a revealing choice of word. Yet despite its affinity with demons, vampires, and monsters, the pipe organ also behaves as the musical voice of Christianity.

It belts out Protestant hymns; it accompanies the Catholic Mass. It provides a soundtrack for baptisms, weddings, funerals, and countless Sunday mornings—a large percentage of the organ repertoire is played before and after services. The link between churches and organs is an ancient one: in 812 a delegation from Byzantium presented a pipe organ to Charlemagne, the Holy Roman Emperor, and the instrument found a new home in a church in the imperial capital. When a local woman heard this organ's graceful tones, she died in a fit of joy. Or so the story goes.

To many listeners, even today, organ music is redolent of piety. This sentiment annoyed my father. Even if a composer was personally devout—J.S. Bach being the foremost example—my father saw no reason why a prelude or toccata, a fantasia or fugue should be heard as conveying any particular doctrine. Great music needs no external justification, he thought; it speaks to the aspirations of the soul, not the instructions of the pulpit.

"A pipe organ can approximate the voice of God," Ross observed, "but it also happily evokes a fairground calliope. It is one of humanity's grander creations, and also one of its more durable technologies." My father played hundreds of organs over his long career, lending the skill of his limbs and mind to fairground and Creator alike. He performed on Wurlitzers and other theatre organs that were mighty enough to make the enormous cinemas of the 1930s echo with the force of music. He played on small electronic organs, not with delight, but with a professional determination to make them sound as good as possible. And he gave recitals in churches all the way from British Columbia to East Berlin. Each of these instruments had a different range of sound—"specification" is the technical term—depending on the quantity, size, and tone of its pipes, the number of its manuals, and the ways in which the manuals and pedals are linked to combinations of pipes. An organ's sound is also affected by the acoustics of the building that houses it. The phrase "pull out all the stops" comes from the organ; it's fortunate for listeners' eardrums that organists never do this.

To describe the methods by which an organ transmits sound is to demand some fluency in a language bewildering to outsiders. One day, labouring to grasp the process, I looked through *Modern Studies in Organ Tone*, a book that lists the factors affecting the quality and power of a reed pipe. They include (to name only a few) thickness of tongue, curve of tongue, shape of the shallot, length of orifice, shape of orifice of the shallot, area of boothole, length of boot, material of tube, and bleeding the boot. The vocabulary alone—a dialogue between Eros and shoe-making—was enough to defeat me. Beyond such tubes and orifices, though, the art of an organist is always one of creative adaptation. A flautist, a trumpeter, a violinist can carry her instrument around with her—Yo-Yo Ma once left his Stradivari cello in a New York taxi. But each pipe organ is immobile and unique. An arrangement of stops that produces fireworks on one instrument may fizzle on another.

This has been so for hundreds of years—organs have a long and complicated history. Start with some basic pan pipes, add a box to rest them on, and build a sliding device to control the flow of wind into the pipes: already you have a primitive version of the instrument my father so adored. The early organ, in truth, is a close relative of the bagpipes.

It seems almost like an admission of guilt. The two most hated instruments in Western music turn out to be cousins. Both of them are wind instruments; unlike pianos, they depend on a reliable supply of air. Once they have such a supply, they can produce a disturbing volume of sound. By the vagaries of history, bagpipes would be relegated to military bands, Scottish country dancing, and the fringes of Celtic folk music, while pipe organs would settle down in churches. Yet organs had been hugely important in the development of European music. "What else simplified the scale and fixed it for ever as a single series of octaves?" asked the music historian Peter Williams. "What else gave us the keyboard, and therefore subsequent inventions like the piano? Probably gave us the very names of music's notes?" For a time, as my father knew, organs had enjoyed high status in the secular realm. In a fourteenth-century

Tuscan romance, a blind musician begins to play a portable organ while a thousand songbirds are warbling in the branches overhead. Awestruck, the birds fall silent. A nightingale pays tribute to his human rival by swooping down and perching just above the organist's head. Then the birds sing even louder than before.

When I imagine my father now, I see him at the organ of the church where he served the longest: St. John's Cathedral in Saskatoon. Whether he was deploying its trumpet and oboe, its flute and celeste, or any of its dozens of other stops, this organ had a singular purity of tone—in the right hands, that is. No nightingales found their way into the cathedral, although one year there were bats. The console at St. John's is tucked away behind a pulpit and a stone screen, a few steps up from the long rows of pews. On a Sunday morning my father would arrive early, changing from his street shoes into a pair he reserved for the organ, donning his blue, ankle-length cassock and a white surplice over top, and checking to see if there were any last-minute changes in the order of service. Then he would stride across the front of the church, stopping to give a cursory bow in the direction of the altar, before sitting down at the organ bench and arranging the sheets of music he would need over the next couple of hours. He owned thousands of musical scores; in his discreet, solitary way, he was a collector.

My father would set the pistons—buttons that control a prearranged set of stops, allowing for quick-fire changes of volume and tone. Then, with everything ready, he would begin the prelude—a stately work, often by J.S. Bach. ("A benevolent god," another of my father's favourite composers, Claude Debussy, once said of Bach, "to whom musicians should offer a prayer before setting to work, to save themselves from mediocrity.") My father avoided very quiet preludes; they were too easy for the congregation to talk over. Lengthy preludes would send me into a state of fidgeting anxiety in case the priest started the service before my father had finished playing. If the priest interrupted him in mid-flow, my father would be sure to take offence. He might get his revenge by an act of musical sabotage. For some years the cathedral had a "family service" that required him to forsake the organ bench for a piano near the congregation, and to play a few popular songs in the guise of hymns. I recall the crowd at a family service struggling to keep up with "Blowin' in the Wind," my father racing through the song at twice the normal pace, his complexion high, his eyes a gunmetal blank. I was mortified—for my father, for my mother, for myself, for Bob Dylan. How many ears must one man have before he hears people cry?

My father's sporadic problems with the clergy had ancient precedents. From early in the Christian era, organs have been a target of moralists. St. Jerome, a Bible translator and supposed lion tamer, gave a fellow believer some firm advice on how to raise a daughter: "Let her be deaf to the sound of the organ." In the Renaissance, Erasmus was equally severe: "Men leave their work and go to church to listen to worse noises than were ever heard in Greek or Roman theatre. Money has to be raised to buy organs and train boys to squeal." The backlash against these noises grew even stronger with the Puritans, under whose influence England and Switzerland saw the systematic destruction of organs. In the 1560s, organs were ripped off the walls of English churches and their pipes melted down to make pewter dishes. A century later, in the city of Exeter, soldiers tore out the organs and, it is said, "taking two or three hundred pipes with them in a most scornful and contemptuous manner, went up and down the streets piping with them; and meeting with some of the choristers of the church…scoffingly told them, 'Boys, we have spoiled your trade, you must go and sing hot pudding pies.'"

Luckily, most of my father's preludes would finish without any clerical interruption. In the ensuing silence he would improvise quietly on the theme of his prelude, avoiding the booming pedals and using modest string or woodwind stops, the music curling and twining and stopping at a moment's notice. Then the priest would appear, announcing the first hymn. My father would start to play at a healthy volume, to set a tone of confident praise and encourage the congregation to sing; he would alter the volume of the ensuing verses by using a different set of stops for each, until eventually the hymn reached a rousing end.

Later in the service, after a psalm or two and further hymns, the choir would sing an anthem. My father would sometimes conduct this from the organ bench while playing the melody. This was delicate: apart from the fact that he didn't have three hands, the console half-hid him from the singers. During a communion service, he would go up to the altar rail with the choir and, after receiving the sacraments, improvise once more, something tender and meditative. The service would finish with a hymn, after which most people took the chance to get up and chat as they shuffled to the back of the church, thin biscuits laid out on china plates in the hall next door, coffee pots at the ready. While this was going on, my father would play a postlude, generally a loud and spirited piece designed to send people off happy, or else to stifle their talk. He always appreciated those few members of the congregation who waited to hear the postlude before standing up.

Such was the natural order of events in my boyhood, Sunday after Sunday, year after year. Each season in the liturgical round brought its own music—Bach's choral prelude "Wachet Auf," for instance, is invariably played during Advent, the weeks leading up to Christmas. Yet my father hated to repeat himself. He always liked to try out new works, both for choir and organ, and no two of his recitals had exactly the same lineup of pieces.

Unlike organists who dazzle by means of superficial effects, my father gave close attention to the structure, the inner voices, of each work. A fantasia, for instance, would set out a composer's main themes and develop them with a rich, flowing grace. A fugue would bring in other voices, their interweaving lines taking the music in new directions before tension was resolved in harmony at the end. My father never reached perfection—what artist does?—but he always strived for it. Music, to him, was an act of reverence and homage. Whereas sermons were disposable commodities, Bach was as essential as bread. Music could be prayer; music could be revelation; music could improve the world.

I found an expression of this faith in yet another of the slips of paper that I came across after his death. Among the piles of letters, musical scores, concert programs, and church bulletins I discovered a typed quotation from the Hungarian composer Zoltán Kodály. It was, I suppose, Kodály's credo, and I believe it was my father's too: "It is the bounden duty of the talented to cultivate their talent to the highest degree, to be of as much use as possible to their fellow men. For every person's worth is measured by how much he can help and serve his fellow men. Real art is one of the most powerful forces in the rise of mankind, and he who renders art accessible to as many people as possible is a benefactor of humanity."

My father might have hesitated to resort to such grandiose words. But Kodály's faith was one that spoke to him. It transformed what might appear like self-absorption into a gift, an act of service. He tried to maintain this faith to the end of his life, sometimes against heavy odds.

8 A few years before I was born, my mother had a miscarriage. She had suffered at least one before. When she became pregnant again, she was told to take great care. Even so, she experienced bleeding in the second trimester. Late in the pregnancy, in the spring of 1955, she entered a private maternity hospital near the genteel town of Leamington Spa, ten or twelve miles from her Coventry home. My father sold his car to pay for my birth. On the rainy, windy morning when I struggled into the world—a long and difficult labour, which left a forceps scar on my forehead that has grown more pronounced over time—my father wasn't in the hospital. He cycled over from Coventry later.

After this harrowing, perhaps traumatic delivery, my mother was told not to risk another pregnancy. She was nearly thirty-nine years old when I was born, and may have received the warning gratefully. I wonder about the effect, though, on my parents' marriage.

I know about its effect on me. Like many late and only children, I grew up with the feeling that I was unique, irreplaceable, a priceless treasure. There could be no replacement, no second chance. There was never any backup plan.

There could also, barring the miraculous good fortune of Hannah and Elkanah, be no brother. I never missed or hoped for a sister. My home already had a commanding female presence, and the last thing I wanted was a new one. Intuitively I felt that my father and I weren't powerful enough to counteract my mother's strength; we could have used some extra masculine force to tip the balance. Hence my forlorn longing for the older brother—always a brother, in my imagination—who had died in the womb.

This longing must help explain my pleasure in the detective stories of the Hardy boys, whose unlikely exploits I devoured. The bookshelves in my Lethbridge bedroom turned bluer and bluer as I tore through their escapades. My mother did not entirely approve. She preferred me to read the familiar classics: *Tom Sawyer*, *Tom Brown*, *Swallows and Amazons*, and so on. Some of the classic heroes had a brother or two. But none of them was defined, as Frank and Joe Hardy were, by the quality of brotherhood. When I grew tired of reading and switched on the black-and-white TV set in our living room, my favourite shows were *Broken Arrow*, in which an Apache chief and an Indian agent are blood brothers, and *Bonanza*, where a wealthy, kind-hearted father oversees a high-spirited trio of brothers. Part of what seemed to make the Wild West wild was its peculiar lack of women.

Why did I hunger for a brother? I was not friendless; most of the time, I wouldn't have called myself lonely. Some days, admittedly, I ended up by myself. I would stand in the driveway, go into an elaborate pitching motion, and hurl a tennis ball against the garage door, hitting or missing an imaginary strike zone and dreaming that I was Juan Marichal, Don Drysdale, or some other star pitcher of the mid-1960s. Easy to pretend I could throw a mean curve or a wicked slider, for nobody stood waiting to cream the tennis ball over the caragana hedge and into the roadway of Corvette Crescent. Pretending to be a batter was trickier: I had no one to toss me the ball. Without question, a brother would have been useful. My father never played this kind of game with me, maybe because it arose from the American sport of baseball rather than the English sport of cricket, or maybe because a hard-hit ball could have damaged his hands. One year a wasps' nest grew beside the driveway. It was my mother who got rid of it.

Beyond ball-throwing companionship, I wanted a brother to take some of the pressure off my rounding shoulders. I marvelled at the family trees I found in history books, the patriarch and matriarch sitting enthroned at the top of a page while dozens of descendants scramble for space at the bottom. A network of veins and capillaries stretches among the lower names, entangling all the distant cousins in a living whole. I regarded this with envy. My family tree was a triangle too. But it sloped down from the canopy of four dead grandparents and arrived at a point in me.

I am the only child of an only child. My father had no brothers or sisters, although his own father buried two wives and spent his final decade living with his house-keeper. Apart from my father, the only male relative I had was my mother's brother, my Uncle Jim. Five years her senior, he was largely a stranger to me. He had been an excellent student, my mother said, but the family required him to find a job as soon as he turned sixteen. He did so, and spent his life within a few miles of his birthplace. Late to marry, he had no children. The brutality of childhood memory means that when I think of him, I recall a man removing his ill-fitting dentures and scrunching up some heavily salted lettuce with his gums in the kitchen of his terraced house. I watched in startled fascination. This was 1966, our first trip back to Britain in five years, and Knighton was as exotic to me then as Mongolia would be today. "You remember Alfred Jones," Jim told my parents. He stared at them, expecting and failing to receive a nod of recognition. "Well, he's dead now. You remember Ethel Price." A further stare. "Well, she's dead too."

Both my grandmothers died young. My grandfathers carried on for years: one died while my mother was pregnant with me, the other when I was two. Nothing abnormal there: in the Britain of the 1950s, any man who made it beyond the Biblical three score and ten was doing well. But as a result of all these deaths and absences, mine was the nuclear family at its most ballistic: a man, a woman, a child. Thank God we had a pair of cats.

Bonanza and many of the other TV shows I watched in Lethbridge gave me an acute, unspoken desire to be part of a large and happy family. I knew the vast majority of North American families included more than one child, and Lethbridge was safe and rich enough that it was easy for me to believe those children enjoyed financial security, psychological stability, and a whole lot of laughs. Or who knows, perhaps a lot of families really were like that? When Neil Gaiman was interviewed for the *Los Angeles Times* about his Sandman series of comic books and graphic novels, he made a telling admission. Gaiman was born in Hampshire in 1960, and moved to Wisconsin in his thirties. "When I first came out to America," he said, "people told me that in *The Sandman*, I'd created a dysfunctional family, which was not a phrase I had heard before in England. I talked to people about it, and I realized that what people in America called 'a dysfunctional family' was the same thing that in England we referred to as 'a family.'"

My older child hurtled into the world three and a half months early—Annie's appendix had ruptured, and the doctors couldn't stop the ensuing contractions. We spent weeks watching Kate fight for life in an intensive-care unit. As an entry into parenthood, it could hardly have been worse. For years we delayed thinking about further children. When Kate was about four, we even bought her a picture book entitled *Lonely Only Mouse*. The book's transparent aim is to help parents reconcile only children to their plight. Thelonius, the hero of the story, has a meek, shy father and a hammer-wielding mother. He envies his twenty-six cousins; more than anything else, he craves a brother. Then his cousin Charlie arrives for a sleepover. Charlie behaves badly. And Thelonius discovers that his guest possesses nothing but a hairless teddy bear, a worn-out toothbrush, and a decrepit little suitcase. Thinking about his cousin's poverty, Thelonius rejoices in being an only mouse.

I was annoyed to find that the author of this picture book had failed to conjure up any more benefits for only children than had the perpetrators of Grade 11 Psychology in Saskatchewan. Thelonius's desire for a mousy sibling struck me as far more convincing than his smug acceptance of solitude at the end. Deep down, I realized, I was concerned about being the father of an only child of an only child of an only child. A year later, Annie and I welcomed our daughter Megan into the world.

9 When asked to relate my earliest memory, I have avoided the truth. I've mentioned the time I was stung by wasps in a pea patch in Sault Ste. Marie, and ran through the garden bawling. Or I've described the summer afternoon when our car broke down in northern Ontario, and my mother calmly read *Winnie the Pooh* to me sitting on a boulder above the highway while my father hitched a ride to the nearest garage. Out of embarrassment, I've skipped over an even earlier memory, probably from the house in Coventry where we lived before our first emigration. I can't have been more than two years old.

I am sitting in a playpen on the floor. The bathroom door opens and my father steps out. He is naked. He hurries into another room. I see his penis and I think, with great puzzlement, "Carrot?"

I know, I know. Sigmund Freud would be smiling in glee.

My father was a discreet, even prudish man. I never again saw him entirely naked. In my twenties, visiting my parents' home in Saskatoon during some vacation or other, I went out for the evening, got drunk with old friends, and arrived back before he had retired to bed. Swaying slightly in the hall, I found conversation difficult. For some reason I used the word "fuck."

"Don't ever say that again," he told me, "or I'll throw you out of the house."

His warning had a comic edge—I was nearly forty years younger than him, a good four inches taller and more than twenty pounds heavier—but in spite of my wobbly condition that evening, I was impressed. He'd reacted spontaneously. He'd made a threat.

This was uncharacteristic. Except when playing or conducting music, my father was not an assertive man. He responded to adversities by hauling them inward. Passive on the outside, he would seethe with fury within. His unspent rage sometimes exploded in rants or took the form of headaches so severe that he felt, he said, "as though my head was coming off." His migraines could last for days. As a teenager, I once walked with him the few blocks from our home to the emergency department of Saskatoon's City Hospital so that he could get some medication fast. I felt self-conscious about holding his arm, guiding him down the familiar sidewalks and across the elm-lined streets, although I knew his pain was so acute he could neither see straight nor stand up straight. I also felt oddly proud. He had dared to admit a need, and now we were doing something together—even if the "something" involved staggering to a hospital. Just the two of us.

The truth is, I think now, he wasn't really prepared for fatherhood. Even if he liked the idea of it in theory, he didn't have much sense of how to go about it. You couldn't take courses in parenting skills back then—you were expected to *know*. He had turned his back on his own father; perhaps he expected me to turn my back on him. But at some point, probably when I was about ten, he taught me how to fasten a tie. We stood in front of a mirror together, father and son, his hands working with mine. The moment registered, it struck a chord, because until then, I realized, he hadn't gone out of his way to teach me anything. Teaching, like so much else, was my mother's prerogative.

She was very good at it. She had worked at it for nearly twenty years before I was born. Then she abandoned her career, devoting most of her energy and intellect to her son—and to organizing her husband's work. She prepared his schedules, kept his teaching files, knew which families hadn't paid for weeks, and made the awkward phone calls to deadbeat parents. In Alberta she did inquire about returning to work in the classroom. But Lethbridge, in the mid-1960s, had no university, and the local school board refused to treat a diploma from Hereford College of Education as a proper qualification. In any case, my father was earning just enough money as an organist, choirmaster, and music teacher to put bread on the table and fuel in the car. Even though extra money would always have been helpful, she trusted that the Lord and her husband would provide, somehow—and they did. My mother disliked being called a housewife but gladly accepted the term "homemaker": keeping each room tidy and clean, writing long letters to friends from decades ago, reading voraciously, and maintaining an active devotional life. She could lose herself, or find herself, in prayer the way my father could lose himself, or find himself, in music.

Along the way, my mother taught me everything from gardening and good manners to the intricacies of Anglo-Catholic belief. In old age she became an external associate of an Anglican order of nuns. When, in her mid-nineties, dementia had scraped away much of her mind, she continued to select the hymns to be sung at the weekly service in her nursing home; she still knew dozens of them by heart. I remember a night, half a century earlier, when she warned me against saying "Geez." I was in the bathtub in Lethbridge at the time. It was acceptable to say "Gee," she told me, but "Geez" was too close to Jesus, whose name must never be taken in vain. I was stunned— the obvious connection between "Geez" and "Jesus" had never occurred to me. Crouching naked in the warm water, I promised to obey. Jesus was, in truth, a name my mother rarely said at all—she usually referred to her saviour as "Our Lord" and to his mother, her namesake, as "Our Lady."

Apart from Jesus, or along with him, I had become the heart of my mother's emotional life. Did my father object to being usurped? He must have done. No doubt this displacement, this quasi-exile in the confines of his own home, accounted for much of the tension that I absorbed through my scalp and fingertips the length of my boyhood. If only he could have found a positive way to step forward and assert himself. But he was too timid or resigned to make any such move. Besides, his vocabulary—rich in the realm of music, more than adequate for politics and football— was sorely impoverished when it came to expressing emotion. Like so many men, he found temporary silent refuge behind a small cloud of smoke. I loved the rich scent of the pipe tobacco he bought when I was a child; those scented pouches of Dunhill and Peter Stokkebye seemed like a proof of manhood, or a reward for it. I was less thrilled by the acrid smell when his match set the tobacco alight. But eventually, to my mother's relief, he gave up smoking. My father was always ready to defer; and, having deferred, to resent.

I educated myself about sex in the Saskatoon Public Library—as far as books alone could suffice—by furtively reading the works on human biology that were, conveniently enough, located beside the books on wild animals that I loved and often borrowed. I would pull *Boys and Sex* off the shelf, quickly hide it behind a volume by Gerald Durrell, David Attenborough, or some other nature writer, and move a few paces away from anything to do with sexuality. Then, safe in the guise of an eager young naturalist, I would scour the concealed pages for information about wet dreams, masturbation, penis size, or pubic hair—information I could never glean from my father or mother. Anyone who saw me standing there would assume I was strangely obsessed by koalas or giraffes.

A few years earlier, inadvertently, I had broached the issue of sex with my mother. I must have been about eleven at the time, lying on the living-room floor as I so often did, and reading the *Hardy Boys Detective Handbook*. I loved the implausible adventures of the two brothers, I loved their social ease, I even loved their peculiar vocabulary—"chums" and "sleuths" who drove "roadsters" and "jalopies"—words I never encountered except in their exploits. But the fat handbook was proving a disappointment. Instead of lifting me away from the law-abiding streets of Lethbridge into some fantastic skein of criminality and derring-do, it consisted mostly of facts about how cops catch bad guys.

At the back of the book, a chart could be filled in. I began the task: name, age, race (!), address, place of birth… The next line said "sex." I was baffled. I looked up and noticed my mother knitting quietly on the couch. "Mum," I said, "what does 'sex' mean?"

She blushed. She spluttered. She dropped her ball of wool on the carpet. It took me no more than a second to realize I had posed some forbidden question, but a few seconds longer before I grasped she was incapable of providing any answer at all. I got up and showed her the offending chart. She managed to give some explanation. I slouched off to my room, aware of having broken a taboo.

When I was a high-school student, and still a virginal one, I came across a *Star-Phoenix* column arguing that sexual intercourse had a single justifiable purpose: the conception of children. I began to mock the columnist—I had grown adept at mockery, even judging Simon and Garfunkel songs according to how satirical they were. But my mother objected: "I don't see anything the matter with that idea!" Again I reeled off in dismay.

Yet a couple of days before I left Saskatoon on my first solo journey—a flight to England, mostly to stay with old friends of my parents, but with side trips to hostels in London and Paris—my mother came and found me at the desk in my bedroom. "Bunny has something he wants to tell you," she announced. I stepped into the kitchen and found him sitting at the small Formica table, his face unusually ruddy. He cleared his throat. He was finding it hard to look his almost seventeen-year-old son in the eye.

"When you get to London," he said at last, "beware of ladies of the night."

10 My father had moved to London as a teenage boy. He knew the city well. But the sources of his misery lie in a small town he rejected to the point of contempt: Knighton, which straddles the boundary between England and Wales near the remnants of an eighth-century earthwork known as Offa's Dyke. An English king ordered the dyke's construction so as to keep the Welsh out. In the 1970s the old school was refashioned into a youth hostel and information centre for the new Offa's Dyke Path, slithering down the border all the way from Prestatyn on the north coast of Wales to Chepstow in the south, and tracing the wobbly line of the ancient fortification. Knighton, whose Welsh name, Tref-y-Clawdd, means "town on the dyke," became the headquarters for the long-distance path. It put Knighton on the map, so to speak. No child living there today could feel so isolated as my father did in the 1920s.

Most of the town lies in Wales, rising up from the wooded banks of the River Teme; my mother grew up in a village a few miles south. St. Edward's Church stands within earshot of the quick water, and belongs to what's officially called the Church in Wales. But Knighton's railway station was built in England, just across a short stone bridge. Any boy living on the English side of the Teme would be, to quote the poet A. E. Housman, "a Shropshire lad." My uncle worked as a railway clerk: he once said farewell to a colleague at five o'clock sharp, and emerged from the office a short while later to find him lying dead on the bridge. The man's head was pointing toward Wales, yet his feet lay closer to England. A crowd gathered. But who should be notified: the Welsh authorities or the English? The corpse grew cold while the argument raged.

Visit Knighton now, especially in the summer, and you might be tempted to call the place idyllic. The high sheep farms above the town have a green splendour about them—you catch your breath on occasion, staggered by the beauty of the rough hills, the valleys, and the restless, mobile sky. Wander down into the streets, and splendour begins to fade. Knighton hunches into its Welsh shoulders, forever staring across the Teme at a dark forest on an English hill. After spending a few days in the place, especially when the air is silver with rain, you might feel on the verge of claustrophobia.

The town has a long and vicious past, little of which is apparent. True, the stonework in the tower of St. Edward's dates from the early Middle Ages. But the rest of the building—it was here that my father began to play the organ, and here that my parents were married—is a bright, airy Victorian affair. Owain Glyndŵr's men once sacked an English castle in Knighton; Shakespeare's sarcastic portrait of Glyndŵr in *Henry IV, Part 1* belies the fear that the Welsh leader provoked. But finally he and his men were subdued, with all the brutality that verb implies. One of the oldest inns in Knighton was famous for its cockfights; today you can play videogames there, and buy curry-flavoured condoms. In the town centre, well into the nineteenth century, offenders were publicly whipped "until the back be bloody." One day, in 1854, a man sold his wife there for a shilling.

But gradually Knighton settled down into the role of a sleepy market town. Small though it was, it ranked among the main communities in Radnorshire—the least populous county in all of Wales. An excellent local history tells me that in the 1920s, when my father was a boy, Knighton had a full supply of eccentrics: an obese rabbit catcher, a stone-deaf milliner, an auctioneer who suffered from St. Vitus's dance, and "John the Dray," who hauled supplies to and from the railway by horse. The year's high point was the May fair. It featured merry-go-rounds, gypsy caravans, sideshows, and a cakewalk: a rocking platform, that is, which gave its users the sensation of a cakewalk dance.

I can't imagine my father trying it out; dancing was a pastime he never enjoyed. Farmers and labourers came to the fair to size each other up. "Want to hire, boy?" If the boy said yes and accepted a shilling, the farmer would employ him through the year.

Knighton had a workhouse too. Eventually it became a hospital. Dark and forbidding, it rose behind the town on Ffyrdd Road. Through the late nineteenth century and into the twentieth, old people who had no other home were dumped there, waiting to die, sharing the building with younger people who were down on their luck or had drunk away their hopes. They wore dark, rough, standard-issue clothing and, unless they were very sick or feeble, performed menial jobs to pay for their room and board. For me, growing up in the shelter of a welfare state, the notion of a workhouse seemed impossibly archaic: something redolent of Dickens, not of my own century. But a horror of the workhouse had been drummed into my father. The idea was liable to arise whenever he grew worried about money or the future. "I suppose I'll be packed off to the workhouse," he'd complain. I would snicker, seeing Lethbridge or Saskatoon around me. He did not laugh in return. I realize now that he always kept Knighton in his mind's eye.

For a small place, it can be oddly confusing. Market Street, which runs into Castle Road, does not host the weekly market. Castle Road doesn't lead to a castle, either. But a castle mound rises east of Bridge Street, which does not take you down to a bridge. Some of the older homes seem to burrow into the ground. I remember one house on Church Road where the front door was less than five feet high. Mabel, an old friend and teaching colleague of my mother, lived there with her two older sisters; then with one older sister; finally on her own. When visitors arrived, the three of them would scurry around the sitting room like aging field mice. Three sisters, living together in a small provincial town, the oldest born soon after Chekhov's death…They used to finish each other's sentences. Only one of them was taller than the door.

But my father didn't grow up in the old part of Knighton. He was born in March 1917, as trench warfare dragged on in France and Belgium. His own father was already in his forties—a business owner too advanced in years to be coerced into uniform. My grandfather had also been christened "Henry." Like my father, he shortened it to "Harry." He was prosperous enough to own a custom-built, two-storey house on the western edge of town. Prosperous enough, too, that after the death of his first wife he committed an impropriety that some Knighton people recalled more than seven decades later: he advertised for a replacement.

I don't know the exact wording of the ad or the newspapers where it appeared. Perhaps my grandfather merely

expressed a need for a live-in housekeeper. But his modest wealth and security must have made him a desirable
catch for spinsters in that small, parochial town. The local
spinsters were out of luck. Instead of hiring one of them,
he chose a young stranger, an outsider from the English
county of Wiltshire; and after hiring her, he married her.
To the end of his life, my father hated how the people of
Knighton had turned their backs on his mother, refusing
to accept her into their tight-knit ways.

That was my father's version. No doubt it's not the whole
story—he was a virtuoso of sour emotion. But it rings true.

Ella Honor Chapman, she was called when she
intruded on the settled life of Knighton shortly before the
First World War. She came from Stratton St. Margaret, an
ancient rural village on the outskirts of the unromantic
railway town of Swindon. As late as the 1920s, Stratton St.
Margaret boasted a firm that advertised itself as a "licensed
horse slaughterer, bone crusher and manure manufacturer,
carcase butcher and dealer in hides and skins…pure blood
for vines always in stock." But Swindon was a different
matter: as the principal builder of steam engines for the
Great Western Railway, it crushed bones in a different way.
I wonder now if my grandparents' marriage wasn't vexed
and complicated by an issue of class. Honor Euphemia,
one of my grandmother's sisters, married well, as people
used to say, becoming the wife of a colonial official in the

West Indies. In the Christmas season, a box of fresh tropical fruit would sometimes land on a Knighton doorstep.

But Ella Honor had not married well. My grandfather was a butcher.

His shop was located in The Narrows, where Knighton's main street rises and thins into a cobbled lane. Philips the florist had his shop there, as did Vaughan the barber and Perkins the chemist. Abley the butcher, for so he would have been known, sold Welsh lamb and mutton and an array of other meats—pheasant and beef, hare and pork—from his premises between Baker the baker and Rees-Jones the draper. It was a sign of the town's prosperity that Knighton could support several butcher's shops. My grandfather owned one of the biggest. On Russell Street, behind The Narrows, he also had a slaughterhouse.

I know all this is true. But I still find it hard to believe. Not that I'm the grandson of a butcher, but that my father—artistic, fastidious to a fault, reluctant to hurt a mosquito—was a butcher's son. Once, as my father drove from Lethbridge to Calgary on an old, little-used highway, the car came over a sharp rise and disturbed a family of ducks on the warm asphalt. One of them flew off too late. My father stopped the car by the roadside and we all got out to peer at the wounded bird. It lay cowering in the dust, unable to move, blood dripping through its feathers. It was my father who took me for a brief walk down the

road; it was my mother who wrung the bird's neck and dis-
posed of the carcass in some nearby underbrush.

After my father's death, I asked her some questions
about his family. Her memories were unusually vague.
One of his relatives had given the newly married couple
some towels and pillowcases, but who? An aunt, probably,
although no name came to mind. She did recall Auntie
Honor, a widow who had returned from the Caribbean to
spend her declining years amid the genteel elegance of St.
James's Place in the heart of London. Honor had supposedly not been well enough to attend my parents' wedding,
"but she sent a very nice carving set. We never did use it
and we gave it away to someone." I must have looked surprised, for my mother added: "Bunny never did like carving anything."

Many years ago, one of my English friends introduced
me to an elderly couple she knew. They had left Knighton
and settled in a Cornish town on the fringes of Bodmin
Moor. Even after three or four decades away from Radnorshire, they could remember my grandparents. But the
memory was a painful one. They told of seeing my grandmother, wearing a white dress, step out of her husband's
shop in The Narrows, her cheeks wet with tears. Annoyed
by her visit, my grandfather had paused his work and struck
her in the chest. Her dress was smeared with the blood of
butchered animals. She had to make her way back to Offa's

Road alone through the whispering streets of Knighton, a local version of the scarlet letter visible for all to see.

My grandmother was "in fragile health" for much of her life. That's the sanitized report that has come down the generations. I don't know what, if anything, the phrase hides. Her lungs were said to be weak. She was only forty-four years old when, in the spring of 1932, she died in a hospital in Shrewsbury, a town many miles away in England. Neither her husband nor her son were with her. They were sitting (so my mother once told me) in the dining room of the house on Offa's Road, eating the evening meal, when a person bearing terrible news knocked on the front door. I try to imagine that scene, and give up in dismay.

Did my father cry that evening? Or was he told it would be weak and unmanly for a fifteen-year-old boy to shed tears? I heard my father shout; I listened to him rant; I watched him fall into a baleful silence and stride off in fury. But I never saw him cry.

It's no wonder I have Chapman as a middle name. What were the odds that my father's only child would be born, twenty-three years later, not just in the same season, the same month, the same week as his mother had died, but on the same notorious day of the week? Ella Honor Chapman Abley died on Friday, May 13. I was born on Friday, May 13.

11 The summer after my father's death, my family spent a month in Britain. For a few days I left Annie and the children to stay with her relatives so that I could explore Knighton. My friend Paul Dunbar drove me there: a poet, a teacher, and a father himself. We camped in a farmer's field on the Shropshire side of the Teme. During the Second World War the farmer's wife—a woman with thick black hair and a shrewd expression—had been a pupil of my mother in a village school a few miles up the valley. Old apple trees, their branches laden with fruit, lined a path to the toilet and shower. Holly berries had begun to ripen in the hedgerows. The only other car in the field was a crimson Ford. Beside its open door, a brush-cut man in a black vest fondled his girlfriend hungrily.

Paul and I attempted to find a chess set for sale. In the ironmonger's shop ("hardware store" to Canadians) I bought a torch ("flashlight" to Canadians—sometimes I feel bilingual within the confines of my own language). On the counter lay a small selection of fruits and vegetables.

"Do you sell chess sets?" I asked.

"No, sorry."

"I thought you might. You sell potatoes."

Paul assured me this exchange left the young clerk bewildered.

A woman working in the local bookshop hadn't heard of either my father or my grandfather. "But I'm a new-comer," she explained. "Only been here twenty-one years. They're just getting to know me." It was the same story in the graveyard. "I'm not a Knightonian," said the chatty woman who watched me walk in, disoriented, "though I've been here forty-eight years."

My name is so rare in most of Britain and North America that I was taken aback to find a generous smattering of Ableys in the Knighton cemetery—seven, at least. There would be eight when Gladys died. I had tea with her: the last living Abley in town, a perky widow of ninety-two who had married my father's cousin. Hospitality obliged her to brew a hefty pot of tea and set out a dozen biscuits on her best china. Gladys lived in a sheltered housing project for old people, conveniently located halfway between the graveyard and the church. She had tales of her late husband. But she couldn't recall anything about my father that I hadn't already heard.

What was I searching for? Not dark secrets, necessarily. Just memories and stories, old news, gossip in amber, to help me understand the man my father had become, the boy he had once been. In a tiny, mobile family, stories are essential: they ground a child in something deeper than the grit and flurry of the moment. I had stories and a few photographs from my mother. I knew how, in her Radnorshire childhood, she loved the purl of running water and the curlew's plaintive cry. I knew how after one late-night dance, she had risen at 4 a.m. to pick mushrooms with a boyfriend. I knew that a discreet pattern of stones lay beside the front path to her family's home, a sign among the tinkers and Roma that this was a house where a weary traveller could receive a sandwich and a mug of hot tea. Yet from my father, I had only silence. And the silence ached.

In the big church near the river, the organ was under repair. I walked in to find it stripped off the wall. Dismembered, it took up most of the south aisle, covered in canvas and multicoloured sheeting. A dozen pipes protruded like long metal bones. "Most of the working parts haven't been touched for 125 years," a workman told me. "Last time it had a partial overhaul was 1923." Soon after that overhaul, my father became a choirboy here and, having made rapid progress on the piano, began to take organ lessons on this sprawled-out machine. It reminded me of a beached whale.

His first choirmaster, piano teacher, and organ

teacher—in short, one of the most important people in his life—was a retired lieutenant commander in the Royal Navy Reserve. H. J. Bray always used his naval title: it imparted a certain mystique, especially in a land-bound place like Knighton, hours from the nearest sea. Even without the title, he would have cut an exotic figure in the provincial town where he spent most of his adult life. A small black-and-white photograph in one of my father's scrapbooks shows a bespectacled man wearing a naval hat above a dark uniform, eight medals pinned to his lapel. Below it is a picture of my young father in a pale suit, his hair neatly parted in the middle, his right hand inside a pocket. Master and pupil, with the master on top.

"The decoration was for sinking a German submarine in the Great War," explained Cecil Rudge, another of Bray's pupils. "After the war was over, he moved to Knighton and opened a cinema. When that failed, he opened a fish shop. When *that* failed, he turned to music teaching. He played the piano inaccurately, in a banging sort of way. For his main job he ran the Labour Exchange. Helped by Betty, of course."

Betty Bray was, as far as I know, his only child. I met her in 1966, after several years in Lethbridge had made me a Canadian. At the age of eleven, I was already at odds with my father. Any mention of the Vietnam War was liable to catapult him into a vicious anti-American rant. After hearing him launch into the topic again in front of Betty Bray, I decided to forestall him by saying, "They should drop an atomic bomb on North Vietnam and get it over with!" I didn't believe this for a moment, but it had the desired effect: my father looked amazed and dropped the entire subject. Childhood, like the Vietnam War, seemed everlasting, and in my unhappiness I was tempted by extreme measures.

The capacious house that Betty had inherited seemed very dark to me, even in the afternoon. The living room had heavy chintz curtains and furniture covered in crimson brocade. To my father the house must have been redolent with memories. My parents quickly silenced me when I followed up my political indiscretion by asking, "What's that funny smell?"

The smell was coming from Betty herself, and the only thing I could connect it with was tinned sardines. In fact it was cheap brandy or sherry, or conceivably both. Orphaned, unmarried, considered plain, betrayed by the love of her life (a visiting naval gentleman who was eventually discovered to have a wife and children in Scotland) Betty resorted to drink. To pay for her morning bottle at the chemist—I wonder how long they kept up the pretence that it was medicinal—she sold off her father's stamp collection, accumulated over several decades. It took me many years to find this out. I grew up associating her name with a sad shake of my parents' heads and a mystery of spoiled sardines.

Knighton has changed a lot since her day, of course. By 1995 it boasted a Chinese takeaway, a video store, and a disco hire. In the monthly bulletin of St. Edward's Church, Father Tim had a page informing his parishioners of the correct way to handle incense. He was writing in the aftermath of a near disaster ("One or two of the choir were almost barbecued"). The regular cooking column was also in his hands ("I have found a lovely pasta recipe"). But in the bulletin's opening remarks he adopted a more pensive tone: "This is the time of year when we start to see strange faces in church, how do we react?"

Some of Knighton's longtime residents reacted to any mention of my grandfather in terms that held no surprise for me. "A bit dour," said an elderly couple who had known him well. "Not much sense of humour, I'd say." "Not someone you could get close to." But Cecil Rudge told a different story. As a young man, he said, he had played the organ at my parents' wedding. Later, when Lieutenant Commander Bray decided to get rid of his sheet music, Cecil had shared out the spoils with my father. His hair had turned white by now, though his sharp blue eyes and gingery eyebrows belied his age. I sat in his fenced back garden and listened to him reminisce. Sunlight swept over the peonies and extravagant roses.

"Your grandfather was a nice old boy," Cecil remarked. "You had to get to know him, like. But I can see him now, in his trilby, walking past our shop regular as clockwork. He walked very slowly. He always thought the world of Harry."

Who to believe? Paul and I retreated to the bar of the Knighton Hotel. "I like a pint of cider on a hot day," the farmer beside us remarked. "Clears your stomach out, like."

I left it to Paul to reply. In my mind's eye I was seeing a slow-moving butcher in a soft felt hat. I knew that my father walked quickly and, regardless of the weather, he never wore a hat.

12 "Come in," she said, "come in."

I was elated. Among all the residents of Knighton, there was no one I wanted to meet more than Mary Cadwallader. She was eighty-six years old and looked a good twenty years younger. Like Betty Bray, she had spent most of her life in Knighton, never marrying. Unlike Betty Bray, she had kept her wits, her good humour, and her health. She made me a cup of instant coffee, poured in some boiling milk, and drew my attention to a plate of cheese crackers ("Sorry, I haven't got any sweet ones"). The big windows of her sitting room looked out across flowering eglantines to the woods and sheep-filled meadows of the Welsh Marches. Books about the region were piled on her coffee table—after retiring from her work as a schoolteacher, Mary had become a local historian. It's thanks to her that I know about the rabbit catcher, the milliner, and the afflicted auctioneer.

Her house stood on Offa's Road, with remnants of the ancient dyke only a few yards away. My father had grown up next door. I tried to imagine the eight-year-old boy he was when Mary, a young woman of sixteen, arrived with her family. It was 1925; already my father had developed the stammer that would beset him throughout his boyhood. He was in luck, for Mary's younger brother Ken took an interest in him, becoming a kind of surrogate sibling. Perhaps it was Ken who encouraged my father to play goal-keeper on the football pitch. More likely not: it was in my father's lifelong temperament to isolate himself at one end of the field, then have to prove his worth by a solitary act of valour as a ball hurtled his way. When I joined the neighbourhood boys at impromptu games of road hockey in Lethbridge, I, too, liked to stand in goal.

I didn't have to imagine for long. Mary was prepared for my visit. She stood up, walked over to a tall dresser, and produced a photograph of thirty-two boys outside their school. My father was crouching in the front row.

An act of kindness to a foreign visitor—although in Knighton, I was finding, I wasn't considered exactly foreign. Never having spent more than a week in the place, I could still be identified and accepted here as 'Arry Abley's son. Now I found myself staring at a black-and-white picture of a building just down the road—a stone building near the Teme, willingly or unwillingly the magnet for hundreds of farm children over the decades, as well as the boys and girls from town. Mary Cadwallader had taught there for a quarter-century. The boys' teacher, Mr. Perfect, was visible on the right. His wife, Mrs. Perfect, had given my father and his classmates their first taste of school, in the year or two before girls and boys were split up and placed in segregated classrooms, entered through separate doors. My father was smiling, very much a part of the group, although a horizontal furrow already creased his forehead…

Mary cleared her throat. I looked up and found her smiling at me benignly. "This is wonderful," I told her. "I've hardly ever seen pictures of my father as a boy."

When my grandfather died in the winter of 1955, a few months before I was born, he left his house and all its contents to his housekeeper and mistress. My parents mentioned rumours of an understanding that after she died, the house would revert to my father—but the will said no such thing. Perhaps this was my grandfather's revenge on a son who had abandoned Knighton, become a musician, and married a woman who declined to eat meat. The house was eventually put on the market, its possessions scattered or dumped. If those possessions included family photographs, they disappeared. Not that my father cared. He meant to turn his back on Knighton, creating a future unburdened by the anguish of the past. He carried the place around with him in his blood; he had no desire to carry it in his suitcase too.

He did hold on to one picture, a single image, of his mother—his mother by herself. He kept it in a pocket of his suit jacket: close to his heart, I'm tempted to say. My own mother may have felt exactly that. It wasn't a *conscious* act of hers to send the suit to a dry cleaner's without removing the photograph. But when the suit came back, the photograph was no more.

Ours is such a visual age that we tend to take photographs for granted. Many people now, no matter their age, never leave home without a smartphone—a camera, that is—in hand or pocket. Family histories are mediated through Facebook albums. Yet through most of human time, ancestors had no face. When men or women died, their images died too, except in the minds and dreams of those who had known them. Only the very rich, the blue-blooded, and the immediate families of portrait painters enjoyed the privilege of gazing into the past—of measuring their own features against those of the related dead. By the mid-twentieth century that privilege had become so common, so reflexively normal, that I grew up feeling cheated without it. Or, more precisely, as I grew older I began to feel more and more curious about my grandparents' appearance. If I'd heard more stories or read any letters, I might not have minded the lack of visual records. But except for the dry-cleaned portrait, my father had not kept any photographs, letters, or other documents from his parents, and he was determined not to tell stories.

I think that's why an ordinary picture—a generic shot of boys in uniform, posing with Mr. Perfect by a school—aroused such emotion in me. It was a window onto something I had always felt to be missing. It was a means of satisfying an appetite long denied.

Then Mary handed me two other photographs: crowd scenes, with dozens of people sitting on benches in the sun. The pictures show the same crowd from different angles. An entertainment of some kind must be about to take place, for the spectators are facing an empty expanse of grass strewn with small wildflowers. Somebody in the distance has put up a parasol. Before the main event gets underway, whatever the event may be, a lady in a white hat is playing an upright piano. The piano occupies a wooden platform. A second lady wearing a flounced dress stands nearby, ready to turn the pages of the score.

"Do you see them?" Mary asked.

See who? I scrutinized the children on the benches—girls in pale dresses and long white socks, boys in jackets and shorts and, in one case, a sailor suit—and found nobody who resembled my father.

"Your grandparents," she said, pointing.

I was stunned. Though I looked and looked, I could find but a single message. Across a gap of more than sixty-five years—for these photographs were taken at Knighton's annual Vicarage Garden Fete sometime in the late 1920s—body language spoke loud and clear.

They're sitting side by side at one end of the front row. My grandmother wears a summer hat and a long, patterned dress. Her head tilts a little to one side—"very typical," Mary was saying, "she was so spry and dainty"—with her hands clasped in her lap. One of her legs is crossed over the other. The top leg, and therefore her body, are turned away from the piano; turned away, too, from the man seated next to her. Under her hat, it's hard to see much of her face, but the thin line of her lips suggests a set expression, as though her mind is elsewhere. She may still be in her thirties. She has only a few years to live.

My grandfather's thoughts are all too obviously there, in the large garden crowded with his customers. He is glaring straight ahead, with a look of greater sourness and severity than any of the other spectators. It could be the heat, I suppose. He has come to the fete wearing a black suit, a high-collared white shirt fastened by a clip or narrow bow tie, and a trilby hat. In this largely female crowd few men are in evidence, but my grandfather is doing his civic duty. The barely controlled anger in his face, the clenched posture of his shoulders suggest that somebody will pay for this later, probably his wife, possibly his child. In one picture his hands are folded stiffly across his chest. In the other he's leaning slightly forward, his hands tight between his knees. In neither picture are the couple speaking to each other. My grandfather is well into his fifties, and he has more than a quarter-century to go.

"Sprightly, she was," Mary said. "But very small." That's not easy to discern from either photograph, although my grandmother looks noticeably slender beside the black bulk of her husband. "She didn't know how to cope very well when your dad had the measles. My own mum was very practical, of course, so she helped…"

It's an odd thing to come across a photograph of your grandparents for the first time at the age of forty. Mary let me borrow the pictures for an hour so that I could walk down Offa's Road to the heritage centre and make photocopies. In reproduction, the quality of the images leaves much to be desired. But as random scenes from a marriage, they tell me what I need to know.

Parade

Over an arch of light I call them home:
my burly, watch-chained, butcher grandfather
taking scant notice of the trout-filled Teme;
his delicate unhappy wife, a music lover,
stepping out as in their fleeting prime;
my mother's devout and tender-hearted mother

beside her husband, once paid to keep the game
on a grand estate and now a gardener there;

all of them radiant, unscarred by blame,
their long-imagined faces no more a blur
until they wave "God bless you" and leave the stream,
broaching the cowslip lanes of Radnorshire

where the darkened bells of St. Edward chime
and the beautiful calamities unfurl.

13　In the early twentieth century, Britain was full of smoky, unfashionable rail towns, the air thick with coal dust and resounding with the metal clatter of steam trains and factories. One of the smokiest, noisiest, and most unfashionable of all was Swindon, located on a main line halfway between London and Cardiff. A sensitive child growing up in Swindon must have longed for clear air, high ridges, and green swooping valleys of the sort you find in the Welsh border country. My father, however, longed for Swindon.

It was where his mother came from. It was the only place, I suspect, where he could reliably get free of his father. A generation before my father was born, the poet Edward Thomas also visited his grandmother in Swindon. Admittedly, he wasn't keen on being dragged off to church there: "The service was a dreary discomfort in which the hymns were green isles." (My father would have sympathized.) But in every other respect, Thomas waxed lyrical about Swindon: "The look of the town pleased me altogether....It was for me a blessed place. The stonework, the flowers in the gardens, the Wiltshire accent, the rain if it was raining, the sun if it was shining, the absence of school and schoolmaster and of most ordinary forms of compulsion—everything was paradisal. No room ever was as cosy as my grandmother's kitchen." My father surely felt the same. And from Swindon, if his grandparents wanted to give the boy a breath of sea air, Bournemouth was just a few hours away.

When Ella Chapman left her family home in the village of Stratton St. Margaret and boarded a Great Western train in Swindon for the journey northwest toward Knighton, I don't suppose she had much idea of what awaited her. She was one of "a string of daughters," either seven or eight of them—but, my mother told me, there were no sons in the family. Having been raised in a perpetual swirl of female company, Ella ended up starved of it. In Knighton her ambitions—and no doubt her consolations—were centred on my father, particularly his gift for music. She hoped he would be trained in the finest Anglican tradition: it was clear he had the talent for it. All his life my father kept a gift he received on his twelfth birthday: a copy of *Hymns Ancient and Modern*, "For Use in the Services of the Church, with Accompanying Tunes." It was inscribed "To Harry, with love and best wishes, from Mummie." Organists who played in the great churches, though, did not have fathers who chopped up animals for a living.

My grandfather was a practical man. His head was good with numbers, his hands with knives. Perhaps he was bitterly disappointed that his only son proved so unsuited to take over the family business. But if the boy's talents lay in grasping chords and arpeggios rather than lambs and chickens, so be it. After his mother's death, my father remained at home for a few more years. Then, in 1935, at the age of eighteen, he left Knighton for good and moved to the edge of London.

The Depression was at its worst. Twenty-five percent of the British workforce was unemployed. It was a desperate time to be young.

Young Organist At The Capitol
Mr. Harry Knight, aged 19

Mr. Harry Knight, who commenced his duties as organist of the Capitol Cinema, Wembley, on Monday, is one of the youngest cinema organists in the country.

He is just under 20. Starting to learn the organ at the age of 12, he soon became assistant organist at St. Edward's Church, Knighton, Radnorshire, his home town.

Then, as a pupil of Reginald New, the well-known broadcast organist, he graduated to the cinema organ, and at the beginning of last year he was appointed house organist at the Regal Cinema, Kingston-on-Thames.

His present appointment is his first solo engagement.

I don't know where this little newspaper piece was published. It appeared in January 1937: the first item in my father's scrapbook about life as a cinema organist. Eventually those items would fill more than twenty pages.

Why did he adopt a pseudonym? It may have been insecurity, or a hope of sounding glamorous, or the urge to have a name everyone knows how to pronounce. Many other musicians and actors had done the same thing. I discover from *Theatre Organ World*—a 1946 book that my father preserved through his numerous moves even when so much else was lost—that, "as most people know, Wilson Oliphant is the console name of Oliphant Chuckerbutty." But I suspect a personal motive lay behind my father's pseudonym. "Henry Abley" was not only his own name, it was his father's. He may also have wanted to create a double identity in music: "Abley" near the altar, "Knight" below the screen. For despite that striking word "graduated," cinema organists had a dubious, somewhat louche reputation.

I think of the lustful organist in Dennis Potter's TV miniseries *Lipstick on Your Collar*. A portly, middle-aged *roué* with a smart car, he uses his privileged position in the cinema to seduce a blonde usherette. From the moment he appears onscreen, wearing a fancy white jacket, smirking at the girl, he's a study in debauched longing. Potter toys with the sexual implications of the term "organist": each pipe a phallic symbol. Yet apart from his wet-lipped predilections, the organist in *Lipstick on Your Collar* is not a very interesting character. Potter depicts him as a weak man, a failure, a buffoon.

Cinema organists were entertainers. They were not so much artists as "artistes"—men (their ranks included almost no women) who aimed to dazzle and divert. Musical taste was a frequent casualty. In the mid-1960s, an English expatriate tried to revive cinema organ-playing at the Orpheum in Vancouver—a rare survivor from the heyday of early movie theatres, it retained a Wurlitzer organ complete with 103 stops. A jovial letter arrived one day in our Lethbridge mailbox, suggesting that my father come to Vancouver and perform a concert at the Orpheum. He should begin, the letter suggested, with a pair of tried-and-true favourites: the Hallelujah chorus from *Messiah*, followed by "Yes, We Have No Bananas." My mother's bushy eyebrows rose in dismay. My father and I laughed and laughed—it was one of the few times I can recall us losing our inhibitions and giving way to anything more than a shared grin, a wink, a dry chuckle.

By then cinema organs were close to vanishing point. But in their prime, just before the Second World War, the top performers were minor celebrities. Cinema organs had emerged during the era of silent films; they survived the transition to talkies because in tough economic times they helped fulfil a need for multimedia, single-venue entertainment. An advertisement from the 1,600-seat Regal Cinema in Uxbridge, where my father played regularly in 1938, promises "Six Great Stars: Two Mighty Films: In One Huge Show." The stars included Joan Crawford and Cary Grant; the films were *The Toast of New York* and *The Bride Wore Red*. Under the movie titles, the following line appears: "MICKEY MOUSE * HENRY ABLEY AT THE ORGAN." My father's pseudonym was short-lived; he had put it behind him. He had been welcomed, under his own name, into the fold of Associated British Cinemas Ltd.—ABC, for short.

The following year saw him promoted to the Ritz, a 2,100-seat cinema in Richmond. If this was still outer London, it was a larger and richer suburb than Uxbridge, and closer to the heart of the great city. Barely twenty-two, my father was making his way in the world. In one of the Ritz's newspaper ads, the names of Rita Hayworth and Irving Berlin appear in smaller type than "HENRY ABLEY AT THE WURLITZER." A black-and-white postcard shows him posing at the console, gesturing at its multitude of stops: a natty young buck in a tuxedo, looking downright cocky. It's a quality so alien to my memories of my father that I strain to recognize him.

Every cinema organist had a signature tune. My father's—"A cigarette that bears a lipstick's traces / An airline ticket to romantic places"—was the 1936 song "These Foolish Things." I wonder if he broke a few hearts performing it.

When a movie ended in those far-off days, a musical interlude would begin. I have a good idea of a typical program because a magazine by the pretentious name of *Kinematograph Weekly* outlined the contents of one of my father's Richmond interludes. With the screen dark and the spotlight streaming down, he started off by playing "These Foolish Things," then swung into "The Lord High Executioner" from Gilbert and Sullivan's comic opera *The Mikado*. He switched gears at that point, playing "Song of Paradise" and "By a Sleepy Lagoon," the sort of sweet, escapist music that had become so popular in the Depression. An upbeat dance tune followed, after which my father ended his recital with the lush, plangent harmonies of "In a Monastery Garden."

Then the great curtain opened again, a black-and-white lion roared, and Bing Crosby or James Cagney filled the screen. Or perhaps the main feature had to wait until after Mickey Mouse had scampered to and fro, or some goose-stepping soldiers and Fascist generals had faded to black. Without either television or central heating, many Londoners went to the cinema for an entire afternoon or evening, eating a cheap hot meal in its cafeteria, watching the newsreels, cartoons, and short subjects as well as two full-length films, and listening to a medley of tunes played on the Mighty Wurlitzer.

Occasionally the organist might be called upon to answer other needs. In April 1939, with peacetime running out, a reporter for the *Richmond and Twickenham Times* evoked "a most stirring spectacle." Every night for a week, the spectacle was staged at the Ritz "as a prologue to *The Warning*, the film showing the various branches of national defence in action during an air raid." The curtain would rise to reveal a spotlighted fireman, nozzle in hand, next to a Union Jack. "Then the light widens to embrace a mass of men and women—hitherto seen only dimly in the darkness—representing almost every branch of the local defence services." By the time the tableau was complete, 150 firemen, reservists, ambulance drivers, nurses, air cadets, sea cadets, boy scouts, and members of the Women's Voluntary Services had packed the stage and aisles. "At the close, at the sharp word of command of Chief Officer R. Barraclough of the fire brigade, those in the auditorium march off while the organist, Henry Abley, plays 'Land of Hope and Glory.'" When the final patriotic chord had sounded, only the single fireman remained on stage. There, as the reporter put it, "He stands guard with his hose."

A month later my father would be transferred again. He became the solo organist at the Commodore Theatre in Hammersmith—one of the largest cinemas on the ABC circuit. It had a capacity of more than 3,100 people. In just four years Henry Abley, alias Harry Knight, had made his way from a small Welsh town to a cinema near the heart of London, one that could seat the entire population of Knighton and a few nearby villages into the bargain. Whether or not this was quite the profession his mother had foreseen, he was fast reaching the top of it. Then Nazi troops crossed the Polish border and Britain declared war on Germany.

14 Early 1940: the "Phony War." The names of Dunkirk and Coventry held no particular significance. "Blitzkrieg" was just a German noun, as yet foreign to the English language. On Sheen Road in Richmond, Bette Davis was starring in *The Old Maid* and Anna May Wong in *Island of Lost Men*. My father had been working in Hammersmith for most of the previous year. Yet the manager of the Ritz had remained a friend. And it was to the Ritz, on March 13, that my father returned. A newspaper ad relegates Bette Davis and Anna May Wong to the lower half of its allotted space. Above their names:

Today Only, at 8:20 pm
HENRY ABLEY
at the Console of the Wurlitzer Organ
His Farewell Recital prior to joining H. M. Forces

This is where the picture begins to cloud. Before long "blitz" would be an English term, "Coventry" a byword for aerial destruction. Entries in my father's scrapbook are scanty now. In a nation fighting for its life, what did music matter?

Again he had a fresh identity: Driver Abley in His Majesty's Army. My father never engaged in battle overseas; instead, as a soldier in the Royal Army Service Corps, he drove Jeeps and trucks laden with supplies—fuel, food, military equipment—up and down the length of England. In the scrapbook a picture of him in uniform, looking improbably boyish, his smile edged with anxiety, has been glued next to an item published in the *Derbyshire Times*: "The annual carnival of Frecheville Community Association was held on Saturday, but on a much smaller scale than in previous years. On Thursday week there was a dance at the Community Centre, and on Saturday a concert by the Mirthmakers Concert Party. The crowning of the Carnival Queen was performed on Saturday by Mrs. Charles Boot." Mrs. Boot must have been a more imposing figure in Frecheville society than the crowned queen, whose name goes unmentioned. "Organ recitals were given during the carnival by Driver Abley, R.A.S.C., who also accompanied the singing at the service on Sunday." This was a far cry from a 3,100-seat cinema near central London. It must have felt like a reversion to his small-town past—which was not, after all, far behind him. The organ was a portable Hammond electric: a successor, I guess, to the equally portable mirthmaker that charmed a nightingale out of the trees in the fourteenth-century romance.

When he had leave to visit Knighton during the war—to see his father, his music teacher, a friend or two, and eventually to woo my mother—he would perform the odd recital and play the odd service. In the autumn of 1940, the program of a recital he gave there identifies him as "Driver Henry Abley, R.A.S.C., BBC Artist to the Forces." That last phrase was thanks to his occasional Hammond organ broadcasts on radio shows like *The Sunday Nighters*. When he wasn't driving around the blackened country, he was taking part in performances of a decidedly unclassical kind, events more redolent of vaudeville than Bach. A "Grand Concert" in March 1942, held in aid of Warship Week at a cinema in Ashford—a Kentish town near the White Cliffs of Dover—featured songs, choruses, recitations, Olive Brierley and her Ladies' Orchestra, and "Moments of Magic by Ciré, high-speed Illusionist." As far as I know, my father had nothing to do with Olive Brierley. But he did furnish Ciré with background music. Proceeds from the concert, it was announced, would help buy torpedo boats for the Royal Navy.

My father was based first in Derbyshire, near the heavily bombed city of Sheffield, then on the western outskirts of London. On at least one occasion, his unit entertained the Services Club in Richmond. "Much amusement was caused by clever female impersonators," a yellowed clipping reads. "Driver Clark as an alluring Mae West, Driver Simon in acrobatic dance, and Driver Witley in songs, where a practised falsetto greatly helped the illusion. There were several amusing sketches, the most effective being 'On matrimony bent,' the story of a tangle in which a charming lady (Driver Clark) mistook a matrimonial agency for a dog bureau." This must be how the Royal Army Service Corps kept up its spirits. Driver Carruthers executed "Scotch turns"; Corporal Lee brandished a ukulele; "Drivers Abley and Duckers were at the piano, and Driver Abley also acted a soloist."

It's one way to serve your country, transporting freight on the road by night and supplying music for crossdressing skits. My father began the war as a private and ended it as a private. But the British armed forces had a separate unit for the performing arts, the Central Pool of Artistes (soon renamed Stars in Battledress), and he did not belong to it. Neither, as a soldier, was he permitted to join the civilian performers of ENSA, the Entertainments National Service Association, whose mission was to amuse the armed forces. The quality of its shows was notoriously variable, leading to the sarcastic epithet, "Every Night Something Awful." My father's exclusion from these units rankled. If it didn't rankle, why would he have carefully preserved part of a letter "written by my friend John (Cpl. Ritchie)" sometime in 1944?

John was stationed in Beirut. He had heard a performance of Richard Addinsell's "Warsaw Concerto"—a patriotic number at the emotional heart of the wartime film *Dangerous Moonlight*. "They had a very fine German piano in one of the places, I wished you could have been with me to provide a bit of *good* music. The ENSA pianist was playing it one day and at my request he played the 'Warsaw.' Brought back some happy memories to me Harry, but his rendering of it was not in the same street as yours. Rather a pity you couldn't get into ENSA Harry, you're a mile better than any I've heard out here." I'll never know how the letter finished. In my father's scrapbook, much to my regret, the page ends in mid-sentence: "There are quite a lot of troops in all male concert parties, some of them are fairly good. I saw a good"

When I was a boy, my father did not, would not, tell me about his own experience of the war. Most of his generation needed to put it behind them, just as many of my generation wanted to learn all about it—the feelings, not merely the facts. I never heard him mention John Ritchie. After my father's death, all my unasked questions hung in the air. He entered the army before his twenty-third birthday. When he was demobbed, six years later, he was a married man about to turn twenty-nine. Those are wide parentheses in a life. My mother told me that through all the years of driving, often at night, sometimes in dangerous weather, he never had an accident—except once, on a long journey through Northumberland and the Scottish border country, he dozed off in the passenger's seat when he was supposed to be driving, and woke up to find a fellow soldier steering the Jeep into a ditch. My father had to shoulder the blame. Yet apart from such rare mistakes and punishments, what did his war entail? A large part of the answer, I suspect, was repetition and boredom. Repetition, boredom, and not enough music.

Things got better, much better, in his final year as a soldier. With the Allied victory in hand, my father could finally begin to recover his vocation. Between May 1945 and February 1946, he directed and starred in five revue shows that his unit mounted at a camp in Hounslow, near where Heathrow Airport would soon devour a swath of Greater London. There was "Victory Variety," produced in the springtime of VE Day; a big photograph shows my uniformed father and a fellow soldier named Eddie Bevan playing a pair of grand pianos in front of the Star-Spangled Banner, the Red Flag, and the Union Jack. A few months later there was "Something to Sing About," with Abley and Bevan, now dressed in white tuxedos, sitting at white pianos on either side of a sultry, white-gowned soprano. Her name was Renée Everett, and she was no Driver Clark. Peacetime would bring further months marooned in Hounslow and further shows entitled "Still Singing," "Yuletide Variety," and "Boy Meets Girl: Prelude to Demob," in which my father seized the chance to spin a little magic with his old signature tune.

The programs and photographs from these revues tell me something. I look at a signed program: "Your music hath charms, Bea Salt"; "Nice work, Peggy Corby"; "As always, Ann." I look at the group pictures: my grinning father invariably stands beside a female member of the cast. I look at a letter Renée Everett sent him after the final show: "My Dear Harry, Well my friend you have done me a very good deed…" By then he had lost his regular stammer. He had also become, perhaps for the first time, a man at ease in the company of women.

Even so, the timing seems peculiar. On August 27, 1945, my father directed Renée Everett, another singer and two comedians in a "Corporals' V-J Celebration" at Hounslow, with a dance band playing until midnight. On September 9, he and the entire company of "Something to Sing About" embarked on a ten-day tour of army bases across England. For the first time since war broke out, the streetlights of British cities could be switched on, and as people gathered in the lit-up evenings the cheap tobacco must have smelled like hope. "Something to Sing About" would be heard and seen by 9,000 people. Yet between August 28 and September 8, my father travelled from London to Knighton, then up to Southport—a down-at-heel seaside resort in northwestern England best known for an amusement park named Pleasureland—and then back to London. He was in Knighton to get married, in Southport for a lightning honeymoon. Those events are not mentioned in my father's scrapbook. Neither is my mother.

15 My mother outlived my father by eighteen years. After her death, as I was going through her belongings, I discovered two letters, minutely folded, in an inner compartment of her final handbag. My father had typed the letters—his spidery scrawl made handwritten letters a trial for anyone to read—and mailed them to her in the autumn of 1945, a few weeks after their wedding. Even though the war had ended, he remained a soldier on an army base and she remained in Radnorshire; months would pass before my parents were free to live together. Two framed wedding pictures survive, both of them taken outside the main doors of St. Edward's Church. They show my father dressed for marriage in combat uniform: a khaki material, belted, trousers creased. He is smiling; my mother, dressed in white, is not quite smiling. One of the photographs includes her father. Neither photograph includes his.

The only thing I recall being told about my parents' honeymoon was that they stayed at a little guesthouse with a red light over the door. Because of the ironic tone in which this information was delivered, I assumed the honeymoon had been a failure. Pleasureland, so to speak, had refused to let them in. Then I found the letters she had kept by her side for sixty-seven years. My father identified himself in them as "Pte. H.T. Abley, 173646," stationed in Feltham, Middlesex—a fragment of West London. Feltham contained one of the largest railway marshalling yards in Britain; it had suffered extensive bomb damage. My father addressed my mother as "Darling."

The letters are, in some respects, typical of the man I knew. He jumps around from subject to subject with no apparent reason or order, seldom bothering to divide his ideas into paragraphs. One of the letters contains snide remarks about a fellow organist: "Sandy is broadcasting from the Regal, Walton-on-Thames twice today. That is where I did a spot of playing a little while ago, if you remember. It is a very nice little Compton there, but I thought Sandy made it sound horrible this morning….But then, he always sounds hopeless to me, no matter what organ he is playing." The letter includes a long paragraph about the latest results of Swindon Town Football Club, a subject in which my mother had a profound lack of interest. Only briefly does my father mention a topic that would have held much greater appeal for her: a possible recital at Knighton. He also speculates about the future of his army base: "All we can do is to hope for the best, and hope that we can stick here as long as possible. The other depots are absolutely terrible—this is like a convalescent camp in comparison."

Yet before tackling any of those topics, even Swindon Town, he writes to my mother about sex:

> I want you so much, darling, that it was probably the feeling of disappointment and, shall I say, frustration, which upset me last week. Can't you still remember those lovely days we had in Southport—I can, and the nights—. You see, when a man is with the woman he loves he wants to be with her, oh so much, and darling, I miss you terribly. I hope you don't mind me saying these things, but now we are married, I feel that it is quite all right for us to say the things we feel about each other, if we want to. I'm so tired of sleeping alone, darling, I feel I can hardly wait until we can sleep together for always, so close to each other, and love each other, oh so much. Please don't be angry with me for saying this in words, but that is just how I feel, and surely it can't be wrong for me to tell you.

The paragraph ends with a shy question: "Do you ever feel the same way?"

Eventually, after informing her about Swindon Town and everything else on his mind, he circles back to private matters. "Don't forget to let me know how the various hairstyles are coming on. I haven't forgotten, you know. You did say that you would tell me. And, Mary Darling, when you go to bed at night, think of me, and of how much I love you. And how I long to be with you, loving you completely, with the whole of my being."

Various hairstyles? Who gives a damn about hairstyles?

He desperately wanted to be with her, and already he was a little nervous that she might take his desire amiss. My father, I now see, was head over heels in love. Reading the letters, I felt astounded, not just at the strength of his emotions but at the directness with which he expressed them. His feelings of love and desire outweighed his usual reticence. "It worries me," he says in the second letter, "that you have to do so much, but oh, darling, I love you so much, I guess I can't help it. I'm just looking forward to the time when you won't have to worry about responsibili-ties....When I am back on the organ, I want you to have a simply wonderful time—you know that, don't you?"

Nothing would come easy in the years after the war. Very little would come easy in their entire marriage. But he couldn't know that at the time. And I'm glad he didn't. Painful as the months of separation must have been, they gave him a chance to imagine a passionate future, shared with the woman he loved. He was young, he was married, he was confident: the future would be rich with music.

By the time my memories begin, my father was neither young nor confident. And one of the reasons for his deepening misery was me. He had enjoyed a decade as the centre of his wife's attention; then he had been displaced.

16 In my father's last weeks of life, Annie went to visit him in hospital. She was struck by the elegance of his hands. Even though the backs of them showed proof of illness—flesh falling away from the prominent bluish veins—his slender, tapering fingers were still beautiful. "They're like ivory," she said. "They're like a woman's hands."

Or, to put it cruelly, they were like hands that had never seen hard work.

His hands were not at home clutching a pen. Before he affixed his name to a document, he would take a couple of seconds to pose his pen at the correct point on the treacherous sheet. And the result would be jagged, uneven, some letters being given unusual weight and others hurriedly passed by. A pen made a poor substitute for a keyboard; that was where his real signature lay. No pen could carry a melody. No pen could deliver a signature tune. Perched on an organ bench, my father had an intuitive feel for the small army of manuals, pistons, and stops he needed to marshal for the sake of music—a different squadron for every church. His hands would flow over the keys as smoothly as a swimmer's hands moving through water. The hesitations, the lurching aches and jolts of daily life died away. His hands grew free. His body relaxed. He became a vessel.

My father's hands were left free for this work because my mother's hands did so much else. My parents adhered to a strict division of labour under which very few tasks were shared. He did take part in the August raspberry picking—after two or three summers in Saskatoon, my mother had transformed much of our back garden into a shrubbery of canes. By late summer, the leaves would glitter with red jewels. She could supply most of her friends with raspberry jam, raspberry pie, raspberry vinegar, frozen raspberries…My father was willing to harvest, slowly. But that was the extent of his gardening. He never planted a vegetable seed, never weeded or hoed or dug the soil. It would, my mother explained, be too hard on his hands.

There was another thing his hands never did: punch or slap his wife. "At least he's never hit me," my mother said to me one day when his mood had been singularly ugly. The remark implied that he had done much else. It also suggested that in the area, and perhaps even the family in which she had grown up, violence against women was normal, its absence worth commenting upon.

My father did use his hands to sign cheques—a task my mother never needed to perform until the weeks after his death. Nor did she sing in any of his choirs; nor did she ever drive a car. But for forty-nine years, she made sure his hands would be well looked after. My mother did all the cooking, cleaning, and grocery shopping—in a marriage like theirs, this almost goes without saying. She also changed the lightbulbs, mowed the lawn, and hammered the nails. Any demands for heavy or difficult labour would be passed along to their landlord of the day. These choices, conscious or otherwise, meant that according to the traditional division of labour still so prevalent in my boyhood, my mother played a leading role. She was superbly competent. Mine was a family in which mother knew best. In some respects she was the man of the house.

For a boy growing up in such a household half a century ago, my parents' lives were a puzzle and a challenge. Other fathers were predictable: you knew where you stood with them. Mine was different. Although he worked long hours, he did not have a nine-to-five job and would do no household chores involving his hands. Having once suffered a slipped disc in his back, he didn't even shovel the snow. He could not skate or play golf; he declined to watch Canadian or American football; he never fished or hunted. He didn't swear. He showed no fondness for beer or rye. He never went out to a bar with his friends—indeed, he had but one close friend, a fellow organist back in Warwickshire. I called this man Uncle Peter, and for years he sent me a letter and a small present at Christmas, but I knew he wasn't an uncle by blood.

Growing up without grandfathers, uncles, brothers, and cousins, I spent my teenage years trying to figure out what a boy's entry into manhood might entail. "Act like a man," I would hear people say. What code did those words express? What behaviours did they embody? Was my father a model of artistic dedication and sober restraint, or was he a sorry mistake to be bypassed at all costs? He wasn't the sort of person who could take me on a camping trip in the wilderness, pitch a tent, light a fire and, as we roasted hotdogs over the low flames, turn to me and say, "Now listen, son…" Manhood was not a state I found it natural to enter; manhood was an abstraction whose qualities remained mysterious, a territory whose borders were inscribed on no map.

My complaint, or more properly my lament, is that even if my father wasn't required for most of the usual masculine tasks, I still needed him to do a few of them. In Lethbridge, admittedly, he and I did invent a game, "hockey checkers," in which round, plastic tokens that came in packets of Shirriff instant pudding—the tokens featured pictures of NHL players—replaced the usual black and red discs, with an adapted checkerboard serving as the most miniature of rinks. To fill the rosters of all six teams, my parents and I ate too much chocolate pudding.

My father loved to walk, and he was never overweight, but walking, organ-playing, and hockey checkers were the extent of his athletic behaviour. He read a fair number of books in his spare time, though not as many as my mother (I found my way into literature under her guidance). In the family romance, my principal relationship was with my mother; my father played the role of a supporting actor.

I spent my first year of high school loathing a compulsory course in woodworking—"shop," we called it—that most of the other boys enjoyed. The girls were off somewhere else absorbing the mysteries of "home ec." I had no wish to join them; sewing was as foreign to me as sawing. All I wanted to do with my hands in school was turn the pages of books and write the scintillating answers. But in shop there were no pages to turn, and the answers had to be made of wood. Stuck with a blunt plane that I had no idea how to sharpen, I fell far behind most of my classmates and passed the course only thanks to the generous, unexpected help of a boy from a higher grade who built most of my coffee table for me.

When I examine my own hands now, I see little evidence of hard work. The fingers are slim: "artistic," my mother liked to say, the same word she applied to my father's temperament. They know how to change a lightbulb, mow a lawn, hammer a nail. But not much else, I admit. I ask myself, from time to time: What have I become?

17 After my father relinquished his uniform, he and my mother lived in rented quarters on a hilly street in Upper Norwood, at the south end of London. Here, far from docks and factories, the unpredictable descent of V1 bombs had left only a few holes in the Victorian brickwork. My father retained nothing more tangible from his six years as a soldier than a pair of standard-issue war medals in a small cardboard box and a formal letter of gratitude from the town of Knighton. One of the medals shows the British lion trampling a dragon.

He had been absent from theatre organs for so long, he could not make an immediate return to the big cinemas in Hammersmith or Richmond. But the ABC circuit wanted him back: they found a place for him at Enfield, on the northern fringe of the metropolis. A few months later, the chain moved him closer into town, to a 2,500-seat cinema in Putney. He was working his way up again.

But up what, exactly? In the 1946 book *Theatre Organ World*, my father's entry heads the alphabetical list of organists at the back—there are advantages, at times, in a surname beginning with "Ab." The book is designed to celebrate an instrument that was still bringing pleasure to millions of cinemagoers and radio listeners. Yet the undercurrents are fierce. An essay written by a London cinema manager describes the wave that was about to break: "The first incentive of the business controller is not how to do more business, but how to cut expenses. Are you, Mr. Organist, sure to survive when that time comes?…Approximately 3,000 people must visit your cinema each week for you and only you, if you are paying a dividend for your employers.…Listen to the applause the next time you ride down out of that artificial halo from the projection room. Perhaps that will tell you whether you would have been missed if you had never come up."

The celebration has the tone of a wake. Cinema organs were no longer being manufactured; television was on the horizon; musical tastes had changed. Worst of all, the nation's economy was in dire straits. Rationing ended in the United States in 1946; not so in Britain, where the weekly rations of bacon, soap, and cooking fat were reduced in May 1945, a few weeks *after* VE Day. Incessant rain in the summer of 1946 severely damaged the grain crop, leading to the introduction of bread rations; sustained and heavy frosts through the next winter, one of the coldest in English history, forced the government to impose a ration on potatoes too. Coal shortages were so severe, few people could heat their homes. Clothes continued to be rationed until 1949, petrol until 1950, sugar until 1953, and meat until July 1954, a month before I was conceived. For more than a decade, even tea had been rationed. The nonchalant ease of civilian life after the war in North America had no parallel in Britain.

Surely my father could tell which way the tide was flowing. If he tried not to, my mother would have enlightened him. Under her influence, he enrolled at both Trinity College of Music and the London College of Music. They gave a crash course in the sort of advanced formal training he should have had many years earlier. By day he studied sight-reading, transposition, modulation, and harmony; by night he dressed up and belted out popular solos at a cinema in Putney. Until September 1947, that is. Then, as he typed in a terse note that he pasted in his scrapbook, "My appointment as Organist with ABC terminates as a result of circuit's decision to dispense with organists due to the prevailing Economic and Fuel crises." A good deal of anger must underlie the words "terminates" and "dispense with." It wasn't quite the end for cinema organs in Britain. But it confirmed my father's swerve to the classical. What other choice did he have?

Unlike my mother, he always retained a fondness for cinema organs. They had represented so much in his life—they had given him such feelings of hope and achievement—he could never look back on them in anger. Yet when I was a boy, he showed few signs of pleasure in any music other than classical. I remember a Sunday afternoon in a Saskatoon winter when my father, unusually relaxed and no doubt egged on by his son, began to play a rapid boogie-woogie tune at the piano: his left hand delivering chords in a major key, his right hand improvising a melody. He did so with easy flair; whether or not any feeling was present, the notes were right. I loved it. But after a few bars he stopped, gave a dismissive laugh ("That's all there is to it, you see"), and refused to play another note.

He seldom wanted to be reminded of the past. Only after his death did I discover he still owned the scores to dozens of popular songs from the 1930s and '40s: Édith Piaf's "La Vie en rose," the Harry Lime theme from *The Third Man*, "Tomorrow Is Another Day" from the Marx Brothers' *A Day at the Races*...One day I unearthed "London Fantasia," a piano piece by Clive Richardson that was, according to a note printed beside the score, "conceived during the height of the Air Blitz of 1940. This Theme symbolises the eternal romance and dauntless spirit of London."

My father had great hopes for *The Music of Man*, a TV series that Yehudi Menuhin hosted in the late 1970s. It

was broadcast on CBC while I was taking my turn to experience the dauntless spirit of London. For several months
I shared a top-floor flat near Shepherd's Bush, where his
letter reached me on a dark afternoon. "The quality of
music is deteriorating," my father wrote. "We have been
getting far too much American bias in the way of New
Orleans jazz, sloppy ballads of the 19th c. and, to cap it all,
BARBERSHOP music. In my opinion, what place has all this
in the realm of music. It would be just the same if Kenneth
Clark had included elevators or tenement slum buildings
in his Civilisation programs." Grumble, grumble. In my
father's aggrieved opinion, Menuhin had thrown open the
doors of "the realm of music" far too widely. Moreover, he
had failed to give the pipe organ its due.

My father disliked nearly all the records I bought as
a teenager, although some of them, from his standpoint,
were more appalling than others. Leonard Cohen's less-
than-golden voice pained him in a way that Joni Mitch-
ell did not; Led Zeppelin upset him far worse than the
Beatles. Such distinctions had a palpable significance in
our house, for I loved to play my records late at night
while writing student essays at the dining-room table.
(There's nothing better, I used to think, than the opening sixty-five seconds of The Who's "Baba O'Riley" for
energizing a dull paragraph or a weary brain. It never
occurred to me that during those sixty-five seconds, Pete

Townshend plays an electronic organ.) The speakers stood on the floor, right above my parents' bedroom in the basement. My father complained only indirectly, through my mother. And when he came back from a trip abroad, he brought me a gift that a salesman at a record store in Berlin had suggested: an early album by the electronic band Kraftwerk. I was nonplussed by the music and touched by the gesture.

The years after he lost his job with ABC are something of a mystery. My father became the organist of a small church in a bombed-out district of South London—but, unusually, his scrapbook includes no photograph of the church and no details about the organ. He began to build a choir there—men and boys only, the ancient Church of England style—while my mother taught in a nearby primary school. I assume she was the main breadwinner. Then in 1949 my parents left London for good. They moved to a village in Gloucestershire so small it must have made Knighton feel like a city. My father took over as organist of the church in Tortworth, a place known only for an ancient chestnut tree. I believe he also worked in the village post office. When I was young, I never thought to ask how my parents had made a living there; instead I wanted to know what pets they had. The answers, as a result, are "I'm not entirely sure" and "a cat called Popeye, who was small enough to enjoy sitting on the palm of my father's hand."

That summer he composed a romantic piece for solo organ and dedicated it to his wife.

But they moved again after a couple of years, leaving Popeye behind in the bucolic torpor of Tortworth and acquiring a replacement black cat named Nicky who would become my first pet: the Ur-cat, the forgotten model for all the other cats of my life. My father took one last stab at the cinema organ, performing on what newspaper ads either proudly or forlornly called "the Mighty Plaza Organ—the largest in the Midlands." The Plaza stood on the west side of Coventry, busy rebuilding after its wartime devastation, and the organ was a four-manual instrument with a grand piano attached. One of the movies playing there in 1951 was *The Cariboo Trail*, the story of an immigrant to Western Canada.

My mother found work again too. For her, Coventry marked a return: she had been a young teacher during the early bombing campaigns of 1940. One morning she cycled to work after an air raid to find that her school had vanished in the night. Policemen had blocked the road to stop people wandering through the smoking ruins. Classes went on in private homes; the English have an under-rated skill at improvising, at triumphing over adversity by quietly making do. My mother did not ask to leave the bomb-battered city, but her father, by now a churchwarden, arranged a job for her in a rural school west of Knighton. She obeyed with reluctance and thereby missed the worst raid, the November night when Coventry Cathedral and much of the city's inner core were bulldozed from the sky. If she hadn't gone back to Radnorshire, she wouldn't have met my visiting father—the unattached organist in uniform, no longer the stammering boy she knew from grammar-school days but a young man toughened by his experience of war.

The Mighty Plaza organ soon fell silent, but a low-level office job at Standard Motor Company proved more lasting. My father was also hired as the organist and choirmaster of St. Margaret's Church in Coventry. It had been under repair for years—the legacy of a German air raid that demolished the south chapel and damaged much else too. Rebuilding took many years. But even if the bricks and stones of St. Margaret's were fragile, the congregation was a healthy size. Here for the first time, amid scaffolding and ladders, my father had the chance to work with a large choir on a sustained basis. In one photograph, he stands at the centre of a beaming group of eleven men, nine women, and fourteen boys. He began to review classical music for the *Coventry Evening Telegraph*—or rather, as in Lethbridge and Saskatoon, he told my mother what he thought about a concert, and my mother polished the prose. He became a freemason, providing tunes for a range of arcane ceremonies while enjoying, I assume, some male bonding. And he became a father.

Even though the Knighton house would never belong to him, my father did inherit some money after my grandfather's death. The legacy enabled him to visit Paris for a few days in 1956 with his friend Peter, while my mother stayed home and looked after me. Postcards from the City of Light show how dazzled my father was. The streets of Paris were cleaner than those of London, the shops brighter, the women more chic—and nowhere in London could you order a drink in a sidewalk café at 1 a.m. The two men visited the Moulin Rouge and other nightclubs. Exhilarated yet guilty at having left his wife behind in a wet English summer, my father addressed her as "Darling" and wrote, "I don't like being anywhere without Polly Wig!"

The legacy took him no further than the Seine. My father was making a modest name for himself in church music, but even when he moved on from St. Margaret's to one of Coventry's leading parishes, the fourteenth-century church of St. John the Baptist, his salary remained small. Without a university degree or a diploma from a college of education, he would never be hired to teach in a British school or become a cathedral organist. Nor, theatre organs having fallen into disuse, was there any realistic chance that he could earn a living as a performer. Overseas, things might be different.

A member of my father's choir suggested he look into immigrating to Canada. And with middle age setting in, my father did exactly that. His departure was noted in a short article—"Coventry organist going to Canada"—that appeared beside a thumbnail picture of him in the *Evening Telegraph*. The next day, a little boy gripping my mother's hand, I clambered up some big steps and we all boarded a transatlantic plane. We didn't have an airline ticket to romantic places; we had three tickets to Toronto, from where we would travel on up to Sault Ste. Marie. It was January. It was an adventure. We were on our way, my father believed, to a country whose most influential and respected musicians were church organists like Healey Willan and Sir Ernest MacMillan. Indeed, had not the young Glenn Gould given his first public concert on a pipe organ in Toronto?

My parents made a decision when they left England: they would change the pronunciation of their name. Through the first forty years of his life, my father was known as Harry Abley—Abb-lee, that is. People in Knighton still say it like that. But when my parents arrived in Sault Ste. Marie, they began to pronounce the name with a long "A": Abe-lee. Maybe my father thought this sounded less abrupt, more musical. Or maybe he wanted to speak his name in a way that would not remind him of his hometown, his childhood, his dead father.

18

The Hardy boys were supplanted in my affection by what quickly became my favourite childhood book: *My Family and Other Animals*, a memoir by the English naturalist Gerald Durrell. I still own—I still treasure—the battered Penguin paperback, held together by decades-old Scotch tape, that my mother gave me as a birthday present in the mid-1960s. I say "my mother" because the copy has my name and address on the inside cover, written in her upright, smoothly flowing hand. The book is a lyrical, often hilarious description of the four years Durrell spent as a boy on the Greek island of Corfu.

As a child I adored his work for several reasons. Under my mother's influence, I had begun to take a keen interest in birds and other wild creatures. She knew and loved British birds, and spoke longingly about their songs; her favourite piece of music was a tone poem for violin and orchestra by Ralph Vaughan Williams, "The Lark

Ascending." This was an enthusiasm I was happy to share. But southern Alberta suffered from an unfortunate lack of skylarks, and my mother was no expert on the birds and plants of Canada. In *My Family and Other Animals* Durrell evokes an extravagant profusion of birds, mammals, reptiles, amphibians, fish, and insects in and around Corfu. What boy—what human being—would not envy his experience of a midnight picnic on a firefly-lit beach, as the Durrell family and a bevy of eccentric friends watch porpoises gambolling through the waves of a warm and phosphorescent sea? Prompted by his delight in every kind of wild creature, I felt privately justified in caring about meadowlarks more than motorbikes.

The book made me hungry to travel, to explore new places, to discover Europe—as Gerry's sister Margo puts it, "A change is as good as a feast." The streets of Lethbridge were straight and wide, the classrooms rectangular, the winters long. *My Family and Other Animals* transported me to a world in which there were no classrooms (merely a few eccentric tutors), where narrow, winding streets held continual surprises, and where the word "winter" hardly merited the name. Reading about Corfu's "hunched and misty olive-groves, up the valley where the myrtles were wet and squeaky with dew," or about "a warm rain that you could walk in and enjoy, great fat drops that rattled on the shutters, tapped on the vine leaves like drums, and gurgled musically in the gutters," my senses came alive.

As the book's title suggests, Durrell also wrote at length about his family. He was, I now realize, unfair to Margo, who appears to care only about cosmetics, fashion, and boyfriends. He was even less kind to his older brother Leslie, whose activities, in the book's telling, are limited to shooting and fishing. The eldest child in the family, Larry, was already a writer—when I read *My Family and Other Animals* as a boy, I didn't realize just how famous Lawrence Durrell had become—and Gerry's portrait of the novelist is more layered and intricate. Yet he makes figures of amusement of all his family, even his beloved mother, to whom the book is dedicated, a woman always battling to maintain a semblance of dignity amid the glorious chaos; and he does so with gleeful zest. *My Family and Other Animals* is a book that brims with laughter, a book in love with the physical world. As a child, I needed that.

I also needed someone like Theodore Stephanides, Gerry's mentor and informal teacher, a family friend who, during the years the Durrells spent on Corfu, discovered three water organisms that would eventually receive his name. An avid naturalist, a doctor, a historian, a scholar, Theodore is the hero of the book—a wise, generous, and pun-addicted man who happily shares his knowledge with a child, never for a moment talking down to him. A few years later, when my own family moved to Saskatoon, I would be lucky enough to find a counterpart—Frank Roy, a high school English teacher who took me out birdwatching every weekday in spring for four years. Through his conversation I learned not just about Prairie birds but also about Prairie culture and history. Frank Roy gave me what my parents could not. He was, like Theodore Stephanides, a warm-hearted enthusiast.

There is an unacknowledged absence at the heart of *My Family and Other Animals*, an absence the character of Theodore tends to obscure. What's missing is any mention of the author's father. A railway engineer in India, he had collapsed of a brain hemorrhage and died when his youngest son was only three—Gerald Durrell might never have set foot on Corfu if his father had still been alive. The book is the fruit of an unspoken bereavement, a loss that has undergone a sea change and emerged as opportunity. What underlies the joyful liberty of *My Family and Other Animals* is a death that dare not speak its name.

As a child, I didn't notice this absence. It seemed only natural. Gerald Durrell was telling stories about a loving, happy family. The people he described, whether Greek or British, never suffered in anguished silence; they knew how to relish the pleasures each day held in store. No matter what accidents or small disasters befell the family or other animals, the Durrells were up for a laugh. They bore no grudges. They told good stories. They took delight in each other's company.

They were never unhappy for long. What place could a father have in such a book?

19 Paul Morel, the adolescent hero of D.H. Lawrence's great novel *Sons and Lovers*, is blessed and burdened by an adoring mother. Trapped in a frustrating marriage far from her family home, Mrs. Morel turns for emotional satisfaction to her gentle, artistic son. I was sixteen years old when I read *Sons and Lovers*, and the novel struck me with electric force. But in one critical way, Paul could not have been more different from me. "He told her the budget of the day," Lawrence writes. "His life-story, like the Arabian Nights, was told night after night to his mother. It was almost as if it were her own life."

Unlike Lawrence—unlike Paul, I ought to say—I did not tell my mother the full story. An incident that took place in my childhood had set the pattern. It occurred when I was eight or nine years old and a couple of boys in my class had begun to make fun of me. This is hardly surprising: I was younger and smaller than them, and little use at outdoor sports. But the taste of scorn was new on my lips, and I told my mother what was happening. Worry lines creased her face; her brow darkened. She asked for the names of the boys in question—and, to my horror, she phoned their parents.

The ridicule stopped. From then on, the two boys avoided me. But the decline of mockery came at a cost: increased loneliness. The whole experience taught me a lesson: Never tell your mother about anything bad in your life.

I knew my father and mother were proud of my work in school. If they were sometimes uncertain about their skill as parents, my report cards assuaged their doubts. After all, Canada was not their home and native land; many things about the country were still strange to them. They weren't sure how to bring up a Canadian son. Their marriage had more than its share of tensions—incompatibilities of mind and, I suspect, body. I tried to do everything I could to make them happy. In high school, when I suffered a year's torment at the hands of a large and subtle bully, I didn't say a word about it. Money was short and my father's nerves were frayed; the last thing I wanted to do was worry my parents. Even when the bully confessed to his aunt and his aunt phoned my mother, I lied and assured her nothing was wrong. The intensity of her dismay was more than I could face.

Soon after the bullying had ceased, I began to write. In a long, narrow bookstore named the Saskatoon News Agency, I bought a copy of Oscar Williams's *Pocket Book of Modern Verse* and sat alone on the grass one bright afternoon in Kinsmen Park, dazzled by what I read. The poems were, as Ezra Pound had promised, "news that stays news." When I picked up a pen at home I didn't express my frustrations directly. But the act of writing gave me a new sense of power. Choosing words, discovering images, shaping them into form, I could escape some of my tensions.

Poetry became an engine of flight—not only from bullying and loneliness, but from overwhelming love. "At sixteen," Salman Rushdie wrote in his short story "The Courter," "you still think you can escape from your father. You aren't listening to his voice speaking through your mouth, you don't see how your gestures already mirror his; you don't see him in the way you hold your body, in the way you sign your name. You don't hear his whisper in your blood."

As a teenager, before I left Saskatoon, I wrote a poem about my father. One day, while he was playing the organ at St. John's Cathedral, a bat emerged from the high shadows above the console and began to zip around the church. My father kept calm and carried on. I riffed on that memory in a poem whose title means "wake up" in English: it's the name of one of J.S. Bach's choral preludes for organ.

Wachet Auf

Above my father's tender head
bats are loose in the light.

He sits at the console, Bach before him.
Each key his fingers pressure
seems to release beasts, flitting, tracing
slits in the stained air.

Sometimes the bats are a grace note, sometimes
a shadow: F sharp in C major.
But they twist now and swarm,
they freckle the cathedral with curt shapes—
a light show whose slides flash so fast
the brain loses grip on its pace.

I crouch in safety near the font; my ears
hear the pure skill of my father
and the pure mathematics of Bach
stumble, discordant. I am afraid
to rise.

And even if I rose

and touched the beads of sweat
studding his head, how could I
stop the bats with their shiver dips
sawing the air as the bars break and the quavers
sliver to a crash
of wings on scalp and fingers clamped to fist:

then silence.

I stole the idea for the last three lines from a Beatles song, "A Day in the Life," where the swelling musical chaos is shattered and resolved by a chord played simultaneously on three pianos, a chord that takes forty seconds to fade away. But the impulse behind the breaking and crashing came neither from Lennon-McCartney nor Bach. The impulse was more private, more personal. As a teenager I wasn't prepared to name my fear in public—I let an image do the work.

20 A dinner party, years later, in my parents' Saskatoon home. I've moved from Oxford to Toronto, from Toronto to London, and from London to rural Oxfordshire, scraping a precarious living as a freelance writer, and I've flown back to the Prairies for a Christmas visit. The house is not the one where I grew up, but the neighbourhood is the same and much of the furniture and artwork are familiar. My mother, having wisely realized that everyone by now is sick of turkey, has unwisely decided to buy some recently fresh fish and an assortment of canned shellfish so as to compile a seafood casserole. The guests include an elderly couple who have been charitable to my parents. Once they gave my mother a side of pronghorn antelope that filled most of our freezer and fed my father and me for weeks. Staunch Anglicans, they are also staunchly conservative.

I'm perched on a hard, uncomfortable chair, clutching a meagre glass of Harvey's Bristol Milk. Herman, a retired businessman with a genial manner and a heart condition, is reclining on the sofa. When the pleasantries are over, he turns to me with a smile and asks: "Well, Mark, what do you think of Mrs. Thatcher?"

It takes me a couple of seconds to come up with an answer. I want to reply honestly but respectfully—to temper my dislike of her aggressively right-wing social policies and her military zeal with a phrase or two about her intelligence and her tireless faith in her own convictions. I want to find an inclusive way of pointing out the extreme divisiveness of her government. But I wait too long. Out of the silence, from across the room, my father says:

"I wish someone would assassinate that woman."

I almost spill my sherry on the carpet. Nobody speaks. For a moment I find it hard to breathe. I feel as though I've been hurled back into childhood: *I-want-to-die-I-want-to-die-I-want-to-die...* Then the air pours into my lungs again, I slip back into adulthood, and I work to smooth things over.

Herman's wife was one of those born-and-bred Canadians who still referred to Britain as "the Old Country," her voice softening in tenderness as she did so. But what she and many other Anglicans understood by the Old Country—what they imagined England to be—was a far cry from the England my father knew. They meant castles, stately homes, Buckingham Palace, Big Ben. They meant the grandeur of royalty and the trappings of empire. None of those items had much grip on my father's emotions. The only time I recall him expressing nostalgia for the British Empire occurred when he found me watching a TV documentary about the worldwide reach of the US Navy.

He glared at the screen. "I thought Britannia ruled the waves," he said.

"Not anymore," I muttered.

His Britain was a land of football stadiums, cinemas, car factories, and army bases—interspersed with organ-rich churches. Affiliation with the Church of England meant less and less in Britain, which was already becoming a post-Christian society by the time my parents emigrated, but it gave my father instant middle-class status in Canada. This brought certain benefits. It also brought certain expectations—a devotion to the monarchy, for instance, and a fondness for the Conservative Party—that he had no wish to meet.

Thinking back, thinking hard, I realize my father did have a few social skills. In the right mood he could be a good listener, an appreciative guest and even, on occasion, a charming host. But everything depended on his mood. It could darken like a thundercloud. And when he was angry or low in spirits, the niceties of polite conversation meant less than nothing. Either he didn't care if other people were distressed by his words, or he had an astonishing capacity not to notice. I remember another dinner party at which he launched into a tirade. I was sitting next to him. God knows what he was deploring or attacking: I could feel the heat in my ears, I could see the alarm in my mother's eyes. To head off further embarrassment, I stretched out my foot and prodded his leg. He stopped his monologue in mid-sentence, scowled at me, and said, "What are you kicking me for?"

"I'm not kicking you," I replied, hating his guts, sensing the amusement of other guests. He had pushed me into a lie, a lie that fooled no one. He had transferred his own humiliation onto me.

I knew, even as a teenager, that my father was free of hypocrisy. He was a very bad liar—incapable of winning the kind of board games that demand a certain agility with the truth (my mother, by contrast, was good at such games, and so was I). When he felt like talking, he said whatever was on his mind. But don't courtesy and friendship depend on a willingness to take other people's feelings into account? At the Christmastime dinner my father didn't care that he was advocating the murder of a democratically elected leader whom his guests admired; all he cared about was his own opinion. His freedom from hypocrisy went hand in hand with a resentful egotism. He was, it strikes me now, a living, breathing example of what Grade 11 Psychology had taught about the vices of only children.

While I'm sure my father felt gratitude at moments, he was seldom thankful for long. My mother was constantly ready to be grateful; she counted her blessings daily. This quality in her seemed to encourage the reverse in him. While he appreciated what others gave him, no gift could ever be enough. "Why is it," Aristotle asked two thousand years ago, "that all those who have become eminent in poetry or the arts are clearly of an ill-tempered and melancholic temperament, and some of them to such an extent as to be affected by diseases caused by black bile?" It was as if a hole had opened long ago in my father's spirit, a hole that could never be filled.

His unpredictability made social gatherings a constant adventure. Even if he didn't blurt out something hideously inappropriate, he might lapse into a sullen silence that people, after a time, found discomfiting. They would glance his way, try to catch his eye, work at dragging him into the conversation—"Isn't that right, Harry?"—provoking a mute nod or a curt "I suppose so," followed by a glare. The fear of what he might be about to say nurtured an unfortunate habit in my mother: she began to interrupt him in mid-flow before he'd said anything offensive at all. On one of the rare occasions when he met Annie's mother, he began to reminisce about life in wartime England. I was fascinated; so was she. But my mother cut him off: "Bella doesn't want to hear about *that*, dear." He shut up then and left the women to it.

It hurts me to confess that my father's rants were not only anti-American, anti-philistine, and anti-business, they were at times anti-Semitic. Somewhere in the past he had absorbed the malignant stereotype that Jews are money-grubbers who pull the strings of power. To attack them was a sidelong way for my father to avoid confronting his own demons. He felt cheated by fate; he lashed out for no other reason. It didn't help that one of his musical peers—a cultivated immigrant from Dresden who founded and conducted a string orchestra in Lethbridge—declared that while Herr Hitler had made some mistakes, he'd been right about the Jews. I eventually told my father that I hated his anti-Semitic outbursts, but he did not apologize. His lack of guilt or shame served only to increase my own. As far as I recall, he never showed any animosity toward individual Jews—one of them, an American who headed the music department at the University of Saskatchewan, was kind to my father, and my father always spoke warmly of him. It was "Jews" as an impersonal force, like "Americans," that he resented.

I'm beating around the bush. My father didn't merely have issues with anger, prejudice, and inappropriate social behaviour: he was afflicted by mental illness. To the best of my knowledge he never lifted his hand against another human or animal; never endured a split personality; never showed any signs of an eating disorder, drug addiction, or alcoholism. But for years, for decades, perhaps for most of his life, he suffered from depression.

Its symptoms could descend on him with terrifying speed: on Christmas Eve, for instance, during one of the major services of the year. I was a teenager at the time, a red-robed server in St. John's Cathedral, looking forward to opening the gifts dispersed around the tree at home. But something—a trivial argument, a grievous memory, an unintentional slight—had put my father in a dark mood. The service got underway as usual; the brightly lit church was full; the choir sang in tune. Then whatever was troubling my father began to overwhelm him. The offertory hymn, "The First Noel," was six verses long. I looked over at him in the third verse when I realized he had missed a few notes. There he was at the console, his face a mask of anguish invisible to the congregation. *To follow the star wherever it went...* Seconds later he couldn't bring himself to play another note: the choir and congregation sang the fourth and fifth verses unaccompanied. With a great effort my father roused his spirits enough to join the last few lines. Probably some people in attendance thought it had all been an interesting "effect." By then my pleasure in Christmas had dissolved like smoke in the night. I was panic-stricken that my father wouldn't make it through the service.

He was hypersensitive to insult. I remember a day in Saskatoon when I was a passenger in his car—by now he had given up the old blue Beetle for a newer red model. Where were we heading? Why was my mother not with us? Time has stolen the answers. What I recall is my father driving slowly along a two-lane road, the car behind us moving ever closer. Its driver honked. My father maintained his pace. When the opposing lane was briefly empty, the other driver accelerated and overtook. Instantly my father lost his temper. Not only did he honk back, he put his foot on the accelerator and slipped his car into a side space on the right that would normally be for bicycles or parked vehicles. He drew abreast of the other car, rolled down his window, and shook his fist at the driver. I cowered in terror. My father was so experienced at the wheel that this manoeuvre may have been less dangerous than I thought. But it reminded me that in his company, peace of mind could not be taken for granted. He never drove like this again in my presence, and I never stopped fearing he would.

After his death I found a letter that my parents' friend Helen Findlay had written in July 1970—a month before the episode in the Bournemouth hotel. Helen had a strong, pure soprano voice, and was a frequent soloist with my father's choir in Lethbridge; she stayed in touch for many years after we had moved away. "I can certainly sympathize," she told my parents, "with Harry suffering from nervous exhaustion. Until about ten years ago I didn't know what people meant when they talked about their nerves; but then I was just too busy, got run down physically and suffered from the same thing. It is a horrible thing, especially not being able to sleep and having to face the next day feeling like you'd been scraped off the floor."

My father must have worried about the candour of his words, for Helen added: "Don't ever apologize for 'moaning' at me, as you put it. It's difficult not to do the same thing back, and then I wonder if there is something wrong with me that I find the two who have followed Harry to be so dreadfully lacking in everything that makes a good choir leader, besides being such poor organists. If Harry had their self confidence and nerve with his great ability, he'd be in Westminster Abbey by now, but then he wouldn't be the lovable person he is."

I never doubted my father's ability. But as a boy, I would have been shocked to think that anyone outside the family might look on such a volatile, unhappy man as lovable. At the time I couldn't hear his whisper in my blood.

I used to dismiss the idea that his headaches, depressions, and mood swings may have had a biochemical basis. This seems odd, in retrospect, because I knew from long experience that when my father was relaxed or cheerful, his eyes would appear hazel in colour, almost brown like my own; but when his frame of mind was sour or he was suffering a migraine, his eyes acquired a greenish tinge. They did this a lot during the early years in Saskatoon, when I was a young adolescent. In Lethbridge my father had quickly found enough students to make a living; but in Saskatoon, a university city full of good musicians, the task was harder. To keep food on the table, he took a dead-end job filing medical records in the windowless basement of City Hospital—the kind of job that digital technology has now eliminated. The work must have been immensely tedious.

My father hated any suggestion that he was to blame for his own misery. But he was, at least, pushing papers in the right building to locate a psychiatrist, and eventually he agreed to see one. My mother had great hopes for these sessions. Nothing appeared to come of them, though— no lifting of his cloak of sadness. He cheered up, to an extent, when the number of music students grew large enough for him to quit the clerical job. But eventually his depression returned. It was like ivy, twisting and curling around his mind, adding a perpetual weight, crowding out all other growth.

For many years I lived in fear of his committing suicide. Maybe this was sheer projection on my part; I was the one, not him, who had devoured A. Alvarez's book *The Savage God*, with its detailed reckoning of literary suicide through the centuries. I was the one who knew how Sylvia Plath had killed herself, and Ernest Hemingway, and Virginia Woolf. I was the one who had, as a boy, kept expressing a furtive desire to die. "I know what you are," said an Ontario writer who met me for the first time when I was forty. "You're a dark-hearted Welshman."

Yet my father had made enough vague threats that my anxiety about his potential suicide never left me. "Not much sense carrying on, is there?" he would say. "I ask you." Or: "There's only so much a man can stand." Or: "I'm fed up with this place—I've just about had it." Consciously or otherwise, he used anguish as a weapon. "I don't know why I bother," he would say. The implication was that one day he would cease to bother, stop carrying on, reach his limit—and act accordingly. Fear of pushing him over the brink was high on the list of things that prevented me from saying, "To hell with you!" and rejecting him outright.

I'm uncertain if my mother shared my fear. But I know that as the years went by, she added a new task to all her other chores: upholder of my father's morale. In the past she had talked about his nerves and his artistic temperament. Now she began to speak more and more about his morale. It was her way of avoiding other terms: depression, mental illness, despair. I would phone their home in the evening, while he was watching television or reading a mystery novel, and she would launch into a long and less-than-riveting description of some minor incident in the last few days— the point, eventually, being that a passing word uttered by the fourth or fifth person in the story "had been so good for

Bunny's morale." This phrase would be spoken in hushed tones, and was meant to elicit at least a few sympathetic words from me. Conversely, any failure or snub, no matter how inadvertent, would be "very bad for his morale." His morale, I came to feel, was akin to the Blessed Sacrament before whose candle my mother reverently knelt in Anglo-Catholic churches: something fragile, sacred, small, and ready to gutter out unless it was lovingly maintained.

What kept my father going was his work as an organist and choirmaster. Even in times of misery he could bring great music to life. And music, in turn, sustained his life. There were sublime precedents for this, as he knew. When Beethoven was struggling to accept his increasing deafness, he thought about suicide. The loss of all sound would leave him stranded in an immense solitude. "Such things drove me almost to despair," Beethoven wrote in his Heiligenstadt Testament; "a little more, and I would have ended my life. Art—art alone held me back. Ah, how could I possibly leave the world before I had brought forth all that I felt was within me? And so I endured this wretched existence." My father was no Beethoven. But the urge to fulfil his vocation as an artist—to bring forth what he felt within him—sustained him even in the darkest, most stricken nights of his soul.

Neither my mother nor I were talented at music. In the absence of melodies or harmonies to reach him, we became conspirators, searching for subtle ways to bolster his spirits. His depression was a prison: although he may occasionally have looked on us as jailers, we felt like fellow inmates.

Music aside, my father spent some of his final years in a solitary confinement of the soul. He would emerge from it, of course, for days or even weeks at a stretch. But when he fell back, all our attempts at reason or good cheer would fail. Those attempts were grounded in language. He was not a man who relied on language.

Depression kept him company in his loneliness. No matter how well his life might seem to be going, depression could be aroused by the next conversation, the next newscast, the next memory. Depression was his silent confidant, his intimate enemy. Depression was patient and infinitely tolerant: it never turned him away.

21   When we woke in the tent at the field's edge, the condensation on the inner roof had come from our own breath. An early train rattled past, heading for the south coast of Wales; then the world fell silent again. Paul and I clambered out of our sleeping bags and trod a careful path through the field—it was riddled with thistles, hazardous to bare feet. Boys were already fishing in the stony waters of the Teme within sight of Knighton's old mill.

Mary Cadwallader had told me about the walks she sometimes took with her brother Ken and my boyish father. On one occasion, nearly seventy years earlier, they had spent the whole day walking. They left the town one morning and crossed the river into Shropshire, making for the remains of a high earth fort known, in English, as Caractacus' Camp. The Welsh name, Caer Caradoc, is more evocative. For Caractacus is a Latin name and Caradoc was a Celtic leader, a speaker of the indigenous language that would gradually turn into Welsh, a man who, somewhere in this wild country of forests and upland moors, made a last and desperate stand against the usurping Romans. Tacitus, describing the battle from a Roman standpoint, put it this way: "When they faced the auxiliaries, they were felled by the swords and javelins of our legionaries; if they wheeled round, they were again met by the sabres and spears of the auxiliaries. It was a glorious victory." The defeat and capture of Caradoc in the face of all those swords, javelins, sabres, and spears marked a temporary end of Celtic resistance to Rome.

Iron Age forts are scattered all over this region, and at least four of them claim to be the true Caer Caradoc. Paul and I decided to climb the one just north of Knighton—the one my father had ascended as a child. We cheated, though: we drove much of the way. We even stopped for lunch at the Red Lion pub in a riverside village named Llanfair Waterdine, a stone's throw inside England, although culturally and historically Welsh. Then we followed a narrow, rising road to Five Turnings. From there the road we wanted, now scarcely more than a paved track, curved eastward. A slight broadening of the asphalt allowed Paul to ease his car to a halt beside a high, fox-glove-filled hedge and still leave room for other vehicles to squeeze past. The prospect of other vehicles seemed unlikely—roads here would have been busier in my father's boyhood. Having emerged from the car with difficulty, I joined Paul and we took a poorly marked path toward the crest of a hill.

Poorly marked, or else by chatting we missed the outline of a yellow arrow meant to show the proper way. As it was, we approached the earth fort along the edge of a huge wheat field that a farmer was in the midst of harvesting. He climbed down from his combine, clutching a sweaty sandwich, as we passed. A black-and-white dog stayed close by his side. The man brandished his bread and meat like a pitchfork: "You're the second party today that's lost your way. It's no good! What do you think the arrows are for?" He was, as people in Knighton say, tamping mad; Paul and I, to use another Knighton expression, felt moithered. But after an uncomfortable minute the farmer relented and allowed us to continue—luckily we were forging a path through the cut stalks, not the standing grain. Scrambling over some barbed wire, we reached the outer ditch of the fort.

Nobody else was there: only a wren flitting among the bracken and the yellow-flowered gorse. We stepped through the outer ditch and over a low earth wall, then crossed a meadow that led to a second ditch. This, in turn, brought us to a high inner wall, now overgrown. Beyond that was the inmost sanctum. The fort looked big enough to house an entire Celtic village; and perhaps it had. Or perhaps the villagers had abandoned their homes in the valley and fled higher, always higher in the hope of eluding the empire's legions, its metal weapons, its terrifying discipline. Flight would have brought the people, finally, to the top of the world, a place of no return and no escape.

A flock of rooks was circling in the lower sky, black against blue. Far below us, the roads were invisible. We had even climbed beyond the brawling of sheep. A good place for a last battle. Now only a cool wind moaned through the grasses.

I tried to imagine my father, a bright-eyed boy not yet afflicted by depression, wiping the sweat off his forehead on a summer day in the 1920s, listening to the wind. It must have been a tough climb, yet Mary Cadwallader recalled the day with pleasure. She and her brother would grow old in the Knighton area. But did my father, still a child, already dream of escaping these magnificent hills and valleys? He could have climbed all the way up Caer Caradoc, the bees raucous in the fragrant heather, summer flies buzzing around his head, a skylark mounting the air, and—no matter which way he looked, toward Fiddler's Elbow or Folly Farm, Lurkenhope or the Black Hill— nothing would have met his boyish gaze except hills and valleys. And so? The butcher's house where he was growing up had the name Hill View.

To the poet A.E. Housman, peering back through the decades from a dry and scholarly maturity, the countryside of Shropshire was "the land of lost content." Yet despite his powerful nostalgia for vanished youth, Housman could be a realist:

> We still had sorrows to lighten,
> One could not be always glad,
> And lads knew trouble at Knighton
> When I was a Knighton lad.

My father was well acquainted with trouble; he had a multitude of sorrows in need of lightening. To my mother this landscape meant the world, but to him it meant a place to flee. There was always a restlessness in him, some inner melody that refused to settle back to its tonic. As an artist, he would be a creature of flight. As a Welshman, he would be angry, later.

He had been dead for seven months, but when Paul and I climbed Caer Caradoc, his ashes were still immured in a box on the floor of my basement office in suburban Montreal. In heavy Gothic lettering, a label on the box said: Crematorium Inc., 1297 Chemin de la Forêt, Outremont, Que., H2V 2P9. Strange to see a postal code in Gothic script. Below that, in capital letters, LES CENDRES DE / CREMATED REMAINS OF—and then, along a dotted line, somebody had typed my father's name. His remains had a number: 248839. Henry Thomas Abley had come to that.

I would have liked to bring the ashes with me to Britain. I would like to have scattered them on the heights of Caer Caradoc. A leave-taking, a good riddance, accompanied by the pure and graceful music of a lark ascending. A return to the green world he had known long ago, before sadness and sickness overcame him. A final homecoming, if you like.

But that would have been a whim of my own, deeply untrue to my father's wishes. He had fought hard to get away from the Welsh borderlands—by what right could I drag him back in a suitcase? My mother had decided that she, too, would pay a visit to Britain that year. And so the box with the Gothic lettering stayed on the floor of my office for two more months until my mother, at the age of seventy-nine, flew alone to England, bringing a heavy carton of numbered ashes to a thirteenth-century stone church in the Wiltshire village of Stratton St. Margaret, now irrevocably joined up with Swindon, where they would be interred in a garden of rose bushes shaded by an ancient yew: far from the Knighton graveyard where my father's parents lie, far from the land of his fathers and everything to do with it, but forever one with the graves of the Chapmans, the earth of his mother's people.

PART II
FUGUE

22 It's early on a Saturday evening in June, and the streets of West Berlin are full of action. I am indoors, listening to a concert. It provides a brief respite from the edginess of the place, where a palpable sense of risk and uncertainty arises only in part from the wall of concrete and barbed wire that slices through the city. Checkpoints to the East are the Cold War made manifest, yet the West Berliners of 1974 appear keen to party through the night—this is a city whose official tourist brochure invites visitors to "join a protest march, dine in faded jeans in a gourmet restaurant, or lie in the nude by the lake at Grunewaldsee." Toto, I've a feeling we're not in Saskatchewan anymore. Berlin's "great cultural tradition," the brochure suggests, "imposes obligations on the city." It goes on to name dozens of German artists, most of whom I have never heard of. At nineteen, I feel more than a little ignorant, more than a little intimidated.

The concert is taking place in a handsome modern church, its walls a honeycomb of blue glass fixed in double-shelled concrete that insulates listeners or worshippers from any commotion outside. It's among the most famous buildings in West Berlin: the Kaiser Wilhelm Memorial Church, dominating one end of the city's main shopping street, the Kurfürstendamm. A hundred or so people are sitting here tonight, many of them looking ahead towards a huge bronze statue of the crucified Jesus that overhangs a plain altar. Behind me is an organ console raised high above the floor as though set into the glass of the back wall. I notice a few obvious tourists in the crowd: introverts with nothing to protest and no wish to lounge naked in the sun. But most of the people in the pews are Berliners—citizens of a split metropolis, inheritors of a cultural tradition— who have come to the Kaiser Wilhelm to hear a recital by Henry T. Abley of Saskatoon, Saskatchewan, formerly of Knighton, Wales.

I'm in the seventh week of an arduous grand tour. The summer jobs I held the previous year, the fact that I still live in my parents' home, and a travel scholarship from the University of Saskatchewan mean that I have enough money to stay on the road for months. Besides, travel is cheap. I've already seen the magnificent cathedrals of Chartres and Cologne, I've wandered the Ramblas and the Alhambra, and in Amsterdam I've sampled the dope and hash brownies in the Melkweg and Paradiso clubs. I try to think of myself as a man. I certainly don't feel like the youth who heard about "ladies of the night" two years ago (many are at work in the vicinity of the Kaiser Wilhelm and, true to Berlin's reputation, not all of them are ladies). I feel even less like the boy who wept outside a lavatory door in Bournemouth two years before that.

This is my first trip to Berlin, and my father's second. Early in 1972 he had the inspired audacity to write to the Canadian embassies in Paris, Rome, and Bonn, asking if they could arrange any concerts. Paris said no. Rome said no. But an official at the embassy in Bonn set up a recital there and another one at the Kaiser Wilhelm in West Berlin. In the end, the concert in Bonn fell through. But the one in Berlin was a triumph. Travelling alone, speaking no German, my father played well enough to be invited back; moreover, he played well enough to impress a tough-minded composer in her seventies named Lotte Backes. She took my father out to dinner after the concert and gave him two or three of her own pieces for organ: jagged, angular works in a modernist idiom. She also promised to arrange future recitals on the understanding that he would perform some of her work. This summer, as well as appearing again at the Kaiser Wilhelm, he will give a few other recitals in West Germany.

If this marriage of artistic convenience raises any ethical issues for my father, he does not articulate them. Frau

Backes is glad to have a friend in Canada ready to include her work in his programs; my father is glad of her aid in setting up German concerts. I was introduced to her a few hours ago, and as I sit near the front of the Kaiser Wilhelm, I can see her grey, brooding presence across the aisle. She moved from the Rhineland to Berlin as a young woman during the Weimar Republic, shortly before the Nazis grabbed power; she survived the Hitler years, the war, the Red Army's arrival; she never left. Sitting beside her this evening is her friend Frau Raphael, a widow who works in a travel agency—Herr Raphael was a soldier who died on the Russian front. Europe's history is all around me here, not only in the city's damaged buildings but in its faces and bodies. My father is staying in Frau Raphael's spacious apartment. I'm staying in a youth hostel.

Before I boarded a plane for Europe, I made plans to meet my father for a few days in Berlin. I wasn't sure what to expect—he's travelling alone again, and I tend to think of him as someone who needs my mother's help to survive daily life. But he has, by all appearances, caught the spirit evoked in the city's tourist brochure: "Just drop into the pub on the corner where the true Berliner drinks his beer, talks politics and escapes for a while from the 'old woman' at home." In Saskatoon my father almost never drinks beer; a glass of sherry or English cider is the extent of his alcohol consumption. But here, as I discovered in a sidewalk café at lunchtime, he enjoys a Berliner Weisse—pale, sharp beer flavoured with raspberry syrup and served in a wide bowl. This is a man I thought I knew by heart.

My father had told me, after his first trip to Berlin, that the Kaiser Wilhelm Memorial Church is the German counterpart to Coventry Cathedral. Only now do I fully understand what he meant. I grew up hearing stories of how Nazi bombs flattened Coventry in 1940, and I knew that a modern church now stands beside the stone shell of the city's medieval cathedral. The new building was consecrated in 1962, six months after we left Coventry for Lethbridge. My father's description of the Kaiser Wilhelm suggested that Berliners had made a similar choice. Here, too, the original building was destroyed in a massive air raid; a remnant tower was left in place while a new church rose beside it. In a gesture of pacifist solidarity, it contains a cross made of nails from the bombed remnants of Coventry's old cathedral. But what I didn't grasp until reaching Berlin is that in its double-voiced grandeur—the injured stonework and the sumptuous blue glass not far from the Wall—the Kaiser Wilhelm is a symbol for the entire city. Its meanings are not purely religious. A monument to the disease of war, the church also makes a statement: that out of loss and misery, life can begin anew. Weapons are powerful, but less powerful than hope. Art can take the measure of death.

In his selection of music, my father is taking a risk. Though he began by playing a work by the English composer Henry Purcell, he immediately moved on to German music: a stately piece by the Baroque composer Dietrich Buxtehude, followed by two of J.S. Bach's choral preludes. A Berlin audience will know that repertoire, and will judge my father accordingly. After the Bach preludes come several works by modern composers, starting with Lotte Backes. The organ is a huge one—four manuals, sixty-three stops, more than five thousand pipes. I've never heard my father play such a massive instrument. But he seems to have mastered it with ease, switching stops and keyboards effortlessly, coaxing a variety of tones from the organ as if he used it every day. A luminous work by the French composer Olivier Messiaen leads into a prelude on a Welsh tune by Ralph Vaughan Williams and a final, brassy piece by an English organist, Sidney Campbell.

"Gaudeamus" is meant to send the audience out happy into the bustling evening. My father, wearing a grey suit and a red tie, emerges from the console and takes a bow. No, two bows. No, three. Confident and poised at the back of the great church, high above the appreciative crowd, he looks as though adrenalin is flowing through his veins. He looks as if he was born for this.

An hour later I'm sitting in a crowded restaurant on the Kurfürstendamm with Frau Backes, Frau Raphael, and my father. Frau Backes narrows her eyes as she describes the Berlin Wall; she doesn't accept it as a permanent fixture of her city; she thinks it will eventually come down. I know this is absurd of her—why do old people always live in the past?—but I decide to hold my tongue. My father orders a bottle of chilled German wine and a waiter pours it into four glasses. I am a juvenile afterthought in faded jeans. My father is the centre of attention.

23

July 6, 1974.

Dear Mark,

Hope you are still fine and well and continuing to enjoy wherever you are. I got home on Wednesday night last. I flew from Frankfurt to Montreal and then direct to Saskatoon. One reason I decided to leave Frankfurt after only two days was because the weather was somewhat wet. Furthermore I just couldn't take to Frankfurt—all hustle and bustle and the atmosphere of money in the air. I wanted to go to the Taunus Mountains, but the weather poured, so I took the train to Wiesbaden (45 minutes)—a very nice place, much smaller and quieter than Frankfurt. When you come out of the station at Wiesbaden there is the usual square of course, but opening onto the most beautiful and spacious gardens which lead right up into the town.

My final night in Frankfurt I decided to have a night out as a good wind-up to my trip, so to speak, and booked myself on the nightclub tour. For the price charged, I thought it was something of a swizzle. The first stop was the Henninger Tower, and after refreshments (liquid) in the revolving restaurant, I missed the exit door and landed up in the Ladies toilet. The last time I had seen a door near to where I was sitting it was the kitchen door, and I thought the exit door was the next to come round—however, it wasn't! The second stop was the Grey Ram restaurant in the heart of Sachsenhaus. We had a wonderful meal in an "old world" type of restaurant, plus accordion and singing. I liked Sachsenhaus district very much— more than I did the main side of the river. (No pun intended!) Finally the tour finished up at one of the nightclubs near the station, which, as you know, literally hit you in the eye. Had wine at each, and I also tried the famous Frankfurt apple wine, which is not as good as Bulmer's cider, I thought.

…Spent the weekend in Bremen at a hotel called Am Wall, which is on a street of the same name, running alongside a beautiful park and onetime moat. The street was originally the old city wall. All this now is in the centre of the city, between the station plaza and the Marktplatz. 600,000 people, but seems very much smaller than Frankfurt—much easier-going and relaxed in atmosphere. Has the most wonderful Rathaus I have yet seen—all that area escaped the devastation of the rest of the city—and thank heaven it did! In the Marktplatz is a very popular restaurant with dozens of umbrella tables where you can sit in peace and enjoy your beer—as I did. Recital went well. Martinikirche is on the waterfront—magnificent baroque organ case. Was removed as an art treasure during the war (when the original 12th c. church was destroyed). I was part of an International Organ Festival there, which is running from May to September.

Sunday night was wet, so I went into the Wimpy where they were inviting people to come in and watch the World Cup on two TV sets. So in I hied, climbed behind several large-scale beers and watched W. Germany and Sweden—also got talking to a young German chap who had come in for the same reason as me. The Schnoor—not far from the Markt—is delightful, a tiny area of quaint narrow streets very much like in York and Canterbury. The old and the new harmonise well in Bremen. The Weser opens up very wide just beyond the city, and so makes a magnificent docking area for ships. Yes! I like Bremen very much!

…Hope you won't be bored by all the "I" talk, but I thought you would be interested to hear about northwest

Germany, where you won't have been. Mum says she is covering news from home for you. Keep enjoying life,

Much love,
Nubbo

August 8, 1974.

Dear Mark,

Sorry I didn't get a line to you with Mum's letter (posted today) which we hope you will receive in Belgrade. The reason I say that is because she forgot to put an airmail sticker on, although the letter was stamped correctly. We dashed in to the GPO, to the sorting office, where Woggo spun her tale of woe.

...Had a letter from Lotte Backes to thank me for the gift I sent. (It was a plaque-cum-plate, wooden, with Saskatchewan flower on it; made in Canada.) We sent a similar one to Frau Raphael. Lotte Backes says that recitals in Berlin are booked up to 1976! but she "has my interests in her eyes"—delightful turn of phrase—so I had better get something going there for 1976. Meanwhile, Wiggins and I think I had better get something going for England next summer.

...Raspberries are doing well—Wiggo has just made raspberry vinegar—freezer filling nicely with heaps of raspberries, and lashings of other things to freeze. Hope your sore throat is better now—raspberry vinegar would soon fix it. Cats are also doing well and wish to be remembered.

Nothing happening in Saskatoon. Sorry this is such a miserable letter, but Wiggy has already given you all news, so that leaves me speechless. Have just finished reading Farley Mowat's Sibir: My Discovery of Siberia—I thought it was a marvelous book—quite an eye-opener.

Keep having a good time—Love,

Nubbo

24 One of the blessings of my life has been the friendship of Tom Murison, an artist and architectural restorer who grew up in rural Saskatchewan. He has an astonishing range of knowledge and an even more astonishing memory. This is Tom's recollection of my parents from the early 1970s:

It was a beautiful summer afternoon when I went to visit you at your parents' home on King Street. I rode my new Peugeot ten-speed bicycle and found your mom working in the garden. The peas were trained high on strings running between little square stakes. The beans, carrots, radishes and onions grew in neat rows with barely any space left between. Flowers grew near the house. Mrs. Abley welcomed me with a great smile and showed me the garden with enthusiasm. I asked if you were home.

"No, Mark is out just now, but he'll be back shortly. Why don't you wait until he gets back, dear?"

Mary had been weeding, and I could see that she must do this every day, because I could not see a single weed, even outside the picket fence. The soil was that rich dark prairie soil, full of nutrients and lumpy when broken up dry. We talked about the garden and then she excused herself to go into the house. She suggested that I talk to Harry, as he was working on the car.

I found your dad standing in front of his car in coveralls. The hood was up, the trunk was open, and a rubberized canvas drop sheet lay under the car. Mr. Abley was just putting a rubber sparkplug wire back on. As he had been changing the oil, he wiped his hands carefully on a well-used rag, and folded it back beside his toolbox. The top tray was out and I could see the wire tool to clean the battery leads and cables, screwdrivers worn from regular use, pliers, an adjustable wrench, and a spark gap tool. These were all the tools one would expect to find in a vehicle in Saskatchewan. It suggested that Harry was one of those people who took better care of their car than the majority of non-farmers, who had the oil in their cars changed in a garage.

He covered and moved the metal can with waste oil and took off his coveralls. I asked him if he always changed the oil in the car. He explained that he did other maintenance too, changing electrical bulbs, checking tire pressure, spark plugs and air filters. He told me that you had to keep the vehicle well maintained when driving sixty miles to give music lessons in a small town in winter. He added that vehicles could develop problems after a visit to the garage, and winked. I laughed because every vehicle my mother took in to a garage seemed to develop the same hole in the head gasket two days after an oil change. This was caused by the mechanic driving a screwdriver into the gasket with a rubber hammer, then waiting for the inevitable leak. No real damage to the vehicle, but steady work for the international brotherhood of crooked mechanics.

Mr. Abley was clearly from the generation who took vehicle ownership as a serious privilege and maintenance as an obligation. When I asked where he had learned to drive, he replied that he had driven an ambulance during the war. I knew from wartime movies of the blitz what this implied. The ambulance drivers were assigned to streets in the area where casualties were identified as soon as the fire brigades had assessed the situation. While this was usually after the air raid, sometimes a second wave of bombing started while the rescues were going on. The ambulance drivers had to drive through rubble-strewn streets, past unsafe masonry walls and raging fires. I was impressed.

Mr. Abley packed the tool box behind the wheel well in the trunk and invited me in. I looked around the garage and saw order and utility in all the items. I was so glad to see this, because we did not have a garage, order, or a father who quietly took care of things that were necessary. The Abley garage was clean, with everything in boxes on shelves or hanging on hooks from the ceiling. We went inside for some lemonade.

Then you arrived on your bicycle.

Tom's letter took me by surprise. I had forgotten seeing my father in overalls, and while I can recall those orderly toolboxes lined up on shelves, I never had the least desire to open them. Nor did I know he handled spark plug wires. Somehow as a teenager I had convinced myself that near-sightedness would make it impossible for me to get a driver's licence—a decade would elapse before I learned to drive in Montreal. In truth, I didn't want my father to teach me. He could have done it, but he never offered and I never asked.

What stunned me, though, was the idea my father drove an ambulance during the Nazi bombing raids. Why had he never told me? Had I ever inquired? My father always recoiled from portraying himself as even slightly heroic. If he did take the wheel of an ambulance, I think it must have been only for a short period, probably at the height of the aerial bombardment, when many English cities were under siege. The men of the Royal Army Service Corps spent most of the war transporting the food, equipment, and fuel that kept Britain going.

After reading Tom's letter, I looked up an official history of the corps. During the blitz, I learned, RASC members "removed debris, delivered water to areas whose supply had been cut off, removed the homeless, and made themselves generally useful." All this came as news to me, although I recognized the tone: a cool dash of understatement in the delivery. North American authors would play up the excitement and downplay the general usefulness. The war movies and TV shows I watched as a boy—*The Great Escape*, *Hell in the Pacific*, *Hogan's Heroes* and the like—starred American actors and ignored life on the home front. Neither of my parents enjoyed these shows.

Tom's letter gave me a further shock.

Another conversation with Mr. Abley was about what things were like when you were very young. He told me there was a regular ritual when he got home from work, that he would sit at the kitchen table and read the newspaper while your mom cooked. And you would come to sit on his lap. So he read aloud most of the time with you close to the paper. One day, he lapsed into silence while he read. You asked to hear more. So he said, "Why don't you read it, Mark?"

You pointed to a line and started reading word by word, slowly, but there was no doubt that you understood each word as you puzzled them out. Mr. Abley said that he and your mother were surprised. But he was very modest about it, and said that you had seen a lot of newspapers and books already, so understood what the words should sound like.

So it wasn't my mother who taught me how to read—I learned to do this on my father's knee? I wish I could remember. I wish I hadn't erased so much.

25 "A change is as good as a rest," the proverb goes, and my parents acted on that principle. They were maestros at moving house. Change was hard: it meant my mother had to abandon her friends and transform an empty space into a home. Change was helpful: it meant my father could avoid facing his demons head-on. But they followed him around. After a few years, when they showed signs of catching up with him, it would be time to move on. Sault Ste. Marie was over and done with. Coventry was over and done with. Lethbridge was over and done with.

My parents arrived in Saskatoon in 1967 and stayed there for almost a decade, a time that saw me through high school and university and on to Oxford. I was surprised that their relationship seemed to strengthen in my absence. Not since his Knighton childhood had my father stayed so long in a single place. But he grew restless. Visits to Britain left him nostalgic for his homeland. The cathedral clergy, moreover, were keen on adding guitar pieces and pop songs to the services. My father made a half-hearted effort to learn the guitar, and soon gave up. Gritting his teeth, he played less "Praise to the Lord, the Almighty" on the organ and more "Joy Is Like the Rain" on the piano.

He was always ready to take offence at a slight, whether or not one was intended. Ministers, in his mind, had the unpleasant habit of proclaiming the Word of God as if music were a byproduct or a nuisance. He resented any directives from a minister that might threaten his work. And in 1977, the year he turned sixty, he decided that his days in Saskatoon would soon be over and done with. He successfully applied for a job as organist and choirmaster of the parish church in Fowey, a little town on the south coast of Cornwall. I can imagine what he was feeling, though I have no idea what he was thinking.

My parents sold or gave away most of their belongings, and re-emigrated to England. Until that moment they had never set foot in Fowey. What they found was a picturesque, hilly town, celebrated by once-famous writers like Daphne du Maurier and Sir Arthur Quiller Couch, with an aging population roughly the size of Knighton's. Sailboats and fishing craft crowd the harbour where a lush river valley, bright with holly berries, slips into the English Channel. The region is superb for walking, something my parents enjoyed, though rarely at the same pace. And the pipe organ turned out to be housed in a medieval church with broad aisles and an elegant carved roof.

My parents were housed in a mildewed apartment above the church hall, which sat at the base of a moist, steep slope. The commute to the organ bench took my father all of two minutes, but when he returned, he walked up a flight of stairs into a home that had, as the vicar put it, "a rather dismal approach" and that was, he admitted, "not a luxurious modern flat." My parents went into all this open-eyed, seeing it as a grand adventure; they revelled in the footpaths, the coastal splendour, the lack of snow and ice, and the quirky grace of the town. Yet the pay was minimal, so my father could survive financially only by giving music lessons; and to serve the limited number of children in Fowey, the school already had a lively music program. After several months my parents' savings began to run low, and dampness in the flat provoked the onset of rheumatism in my father's wrists. He sent urgent letters to Saskatoon in hopes of finding another job. Amazingly, he found two.

A year after my parents left Saskatchewan, they moved back. In the dry climate of the Prairies, my father's rheumatism cleared up at once. Now he was the organist and choirmaster of a small Anglican church on the south side of Saskatoon where the main service started at 10 a.m., as well as a hulking United church downtown where worship began an hour later. Each Sunday, regardless of the weather, he would play a prelude and the first half hour of the All Saints service, then dash to his car and take the freeway over the South Saskatchewan River in time, with luck, to don a new set of robes, climb into the organ loft, and perform a prelude in the stone edifice of Third Avenue United. He was also named Instructor in Organ for music students at the University of Saskatchewan—a title he relished, given that he had left school as a teenager.

It took a long while for my parents to find the right place to live. They spent a few months in a furnished house while their remaining belongings were chugging slowly back across the North Atlantic; then they moved into an apartment whose landlord reduced the rent because my mother agreed to clean his home; then they rented a bungalow on the far side of town; then, at last, they settled in a two-storey house in their original neighbourhood, a stone's throw from Kinsmen Park and the pelican-busy river. The house was a rental property owned by an old friend and mentor of mine. My parents never knew that at the age of twenty-five, as a freelance writer in England with small savings and no security, I kept their rent artificially low by mailing my friend a quarterly cheque. I was worried about my parents. Already I felt responsible.

The next few years, in artistic terms, were the busiest and best of my father's life. His talents, at last, were widely recognized. Eric Burt, a fellow member of the Mystic Tie Masonic lodge and a reporter for the *Saskatoon Star-Phoenix*, wrote about my father in several appreciative articles. "His many friends," Burt declared in 1980, "think he hasn't been in the headlines enough. They see him as modest and unassuming. He admits a feeling of insecurity." Burt reminded my father that one of his anthems for choir and organ, "Jubilate Deo," had been sung in St. John's Cathedral a few years earlier when the Archbishop of Canterbury swept through town. My father's reaction was defensive, as though Burt had accused him of putting himself forward: "I didn't force it on the choir. It was requested by the Bishop of Saskatoon." A different composer—a different man—would have said, "That's right, Eric, and don't forget I also wrote a processional fanfare for trumpets and organ to welcome the Archbishop."

Feet on pedals, fingers on manuals, eyes on the score in front of him, no insecurity was evident. And it seemed, in the early 1980s, as if my father was finally earning the acclaim he was shy to admit he craved. I organized concerts for him in Oxford and Cambridge. Lotte Backes arranged tours for him in Germany, where he now travelled with my mother by his side. One year he obtained a visa to play a concert in a large church in East Berlin. After the recital my parents caught a train to Leipzig, the home of J.S. Bach for much of his adult life, making a pilgrimage to St. Thomas's Church and the composer's unassuming grave.

The city of Saskatoon launched Canada Music Week in 1981 with a concert devoted to my father's compositions, featuring three choirs, a soprano soloist, a violinist, a band, a trumpet trio, a string trio—and himself at the pipe organ, of course. That fall he played a concert on CBC Radio's *Organists in Recital*, broadcast across the country. His choice of music was uncompromising: four twentieth-century pieces, one of them highly discordant. (That was a work by Lotte Backes.) My father also included a personal favourite, "Le Jardin Suspendu," written by a French composer, Jehan Alain, who died young in the Second World War. It's a brooding, mysterious work, which Alain described as "an expression of the artist's ideal—perpetually sought, elusive, yet becoming his refuge, inaccessible and inviolable."

In music my father discovered his refuge. Playing the organ, leading a choir, teaching students, he felt justified. This was what he was trained to do and what he loved to do above all else. Music allowed him to feel useful in the world. Inaccessible and inviolable, it kept depression at bay.

26 My father was useless in the kitchen. He repaired nothing in the house. He never accumulated much money. As I watched him sitting at the dining-room table, both of us waiting for my mother to bring food, I judged him. He was, I decided as a boy, the most impractical man on the face of the Earth. (I chose to ignore the spark plugs and the oil changes.) An artistic temperament, surely, was at odds with practical life.

Decades later, as I browse through the scores of his compositions, I realize they are models of practicality. My father's music reveals a consistent pragmatism, a willingness to adapt to local means. His adaptation of the "Huron Carol," for instance, was dedicated "to my friends of Third Avenue United church choir, Saskatoon." The carol "should be sung freely," he wrote, "and unaccompanied (preferably) except where the organ is indicated, but it can be accompanied all through, of course." My father must have hoped the carol would be heard elsewhere too, for he noted that "the men's part is kept simple deliberately, in order to accommodate the universal shortage of men in choirs." He harmonized the familiar tune and arranged it for flute and organ—adding, however, that "If a flautist is not available, the flute part would have to be played on the organ."

Eight years later, preparing a new anthem to be sung by the small choir at his final church, he arranged an ancient English carol, "Tomorrow shall be my dancing day." "It may be sung by voices in unison," he explained in a note; "or in two parts (soprano and baritone); or in three parts (soprano, alto and baritone). The voice parts may be accompanied (organ or piano), or unaccompanied." An alternative setting for the second verse inverts the soprano line, allowing the baritone to sing the melody. The aim is maximum versatility for a minimum of voices. It's as if the constraints imposed by a dearth of resources served to spur his imagination.

My father produced a variety of settings for the chanted psalms and prayers that form (or used to form) a central part of Anglican communion services. The last of these, "A Mass for Unison Voices and Organ," is written in the plainest of styles, to serve a congregation and a little choir that would have trouble coping with any melodic leaps or harmonic complexities. It takes the often unpoetic words found in the 1985 *Book of Alternative Services* and turns them into something approaching beauty. My father was a lifelong Anglican. But he was more than willing to turn his hand to the language of other traditions too. Visiting Oxford when I was a student there, he met a friend of mine—a rugby-playing monk from Australia—who had written simple melodies for the Roman Catholic Mass; my father harmonized them. During the last year of his life, for reasons that elude me, he composed a liturgical sequence for the United Church of Canada.

His pragmatism, I now see, was a distant, minor echo of a similar trait in his lifelong hero. J.S. Bach also earned his living as an organist, choirmaster, and music teacher, and he, too, would modify his inspirations according to the instruments and choirs at his disposal. Liszt and Paganini, Ravel and Rachmaninov wrote music that the most gifted performers have found all but unplayable. Bach never did this. Many of his pieces pose a technical challenge, yet a generosity of spirit prevented him from asking the impossible of musicians. One of Bach's qualities that my father most appreciated was his practicality.

The feeling that emerges most clearly from my father's work is a restrained yet heartfelt yearning. His music never sounds blunt, edgy, sardonic. However bitter he could be in person, his compositions are devoid of bitterness. It's as if he poured a sweetness of spirit into his art, leaving the acid for daily life. In Saskatoon he set a poem by Christina

Rossetti to music: "Love Came Down at Christmas." In twelve lines, it uses the word "love" eleven times and "lovely" once. My father's setting asks for a solo soprano, a choir, and an organ accompaniment. A direction says: "Gently and simply." "Petite Rhapsodie" for piano is subtitled "Sous les étoiles" and bears an instruction in Italian: "piangevole e con amore." Plaintively, that is, and with love. His earliest composition that I know of—"Meditation," for organ solo—begins quietly, scored for soft reed and tremulant, and ends even more quietly, scored for soft flute. He wrote the piece in rural Gloucestershire in July 1949, and dedicated it "To Mary." It's a love letter, spelled out in the melodic language of his hands and heart.

To the world at large, these are not important pieces of music. But they're important to me, for they reveal the kind of spirit my father had, beyond the anguish that beset him. He limited himself to what he could do well; he never tried to compose a symphony or a string quartet. With a pencil behind his ear and a blank score on the music stand, he was both a practical man and a romantic.

In his personal habits he remained forever English. The cuisines that now dominate restaurant menus throughout the Western world—Indian, Chinese, Italian, Greek, Japanese—held no appeal for him. His clothing was conservative and unadventurous in style, and he had no ear for foreign languages—when the poet Anne Szumigalski once phoned and left a message for me, he scribbled a note saying that Angela McGowsky had called. But music, once again, was another story. My father found catalysts anywhere and everywhere. A "Folk Tune Suite" that he arranged and harmonized for piano has melodies not only from Wales and England but also from Ukraine, Russia, Czechoslovakia, and Quebec. He adapted the Baptist hymn "How Firm a Foundation" to a tune from the American South, and gave an Easter lyric written by an eighth-century saint the melody of a Provençal carol.

My father's political views are discernible in a few of these pieces, expressed in their most positive, good-natured manner. The rage and frustration that so often spilled over when he talked about politics are nowhere to be heard in his music. Most of the texts that inspired his choral music are Christian, of course. But not all. There's nothing Christian about the four stanzas of "These Things Shall Be," a poem by the Victorian writer J.A. Symonds:

Nation with nation, land with land,
Unarmed shall live as comrades free;
In ev'ry heart and brain shall throb
The pulse of one fraternity.

Somewhere my father unearthed a "Credo" with words supposedly translated from the Chinese: "I believe in the living friendship given by flowers and trees: / Outwardly they die, but in the heart they live for ever..." He set "Credo" to music too, as he did some ancient verses known as "The Flower Carol"—a carol for spring, not winter. It expresses a passionate joy in nature that over the long centuries the church has often struggled to accept:

> All the world with beauty fills,
> Gold the green enhancing;
> Flowers make glee among the hills
> And set the meadows dancing.

This carol would have held tremendous appeal for my father because of how it describes God: not a maker of laws, not an enforcer of rules, but an "artist without rival."

Through the passing years, many of his piano students were the recipient of a gift: a morsel of new music. With a mixture of realism and tact, my father tailored each composition to the level the student had reached. For a girl in Saskatoon he wrote "The Song of a Graceful Heart"—a lyrical piece that he identified as a romance. To the daughter of the parish priest in Fowey he gave "A Children's Suite," five short piano pieces including a march and a "merry dance." Back in Saskatoon he composed at least eight more pieces for children, one of them, "Chelsea Reach," dedicated to an idealistic girl who was his particular favourite.

I suspect he also created "Free Spirit" with her in mind. It's a short work for piano in G-flat major, a key of six flats. Schubert and Chopin wrote impromptus in G-flat major, and Debussy used it in a tender, evocative piece my father loved: "La Fille aux cheveux de lin." The key is a tricky one to play, and the handwritten score of "Free Spirit" is packed with Italian and Latin terms I don't immediately recognize: *slentando*, *meno mosso*, *ad libitum*. Has anybody except my father ever played it?

27

January 25, 1981.

Dear Mark,

Sorry to be longer than I had wanted to be in writing, but the time flies, and there always seems to be something cropping up which has to be seen to immediately. Such as getting a teaching curriculum off to the university; telephoning organ companies re a new console; setting up my Spring series of concerts; meetings with Al Gaspar's various wretched committees; getting flu; and sundry other things; so that it no sooner becomes Monday than it's Saturday again. However, I wasn't upset by your first letter and its salutary remarks! Of course, you are quite right in saying "Ease up" at my age, and I really do appreciate your concern. But don't you worry! There is nothing to worry about. I am fine, feeling good, and enjoying what I'm doing. My students must surely be the best lot I've ever had, and I love them all; plus the fact that I think my work is appreciated at both 3rd Avenue and All Saints; added to which there is you and Mum rooting for me all the time, so when one comes to think of it, I'm pretty lucky!

…At the moment I am engaged in writing a piano duet (a march) for two of my little students, the Hyslop twins, and am also in the middle of an organ piece based on the French tune "O Quanta Qualia"; nothing special, but adequate, I hope. Apparently my "Jubilate Deo" was sung by Zion Lutheran Choir over cable TV here last month, unbeknown to me! I was furious, because they obviously had it xeroxed without asking me, and then without even asking me how it was to be performed. So I just hope they didn't make a complete hash of it! Helen Pridmore is going to sing my two songs over the same TV next month, and I've been asked to go on and be interviewed. Heaven help us all! Can you imagine me talking on TV. I'm terrified, for one thing, and shall feel completely ridiculous for another.…

Much love to you both,
Nubbo
In a hurry, as always

May 2, 1981.

Dear Mark,

Please forgive the awfully long time I've been in writing
to you this time, but Mum has told you that I really
have been run off my feet for the last couple of months.
It reached the stage of taking each thing as it came
along, day by day, without being able to look ahead
even to the next thing which was coming up. I had
two weeks only in which to learn the music for the
University Chorus concert, with one rehearsal only,
and this included 53 pages of Liszt's "Missa Choralis,"
plus a bunch of other stuff which had to have organ
accompaniment—the two American pieces were very
difficult, to say the least, and the Liszt one for male
voices was a real weirdo—all 7th dissonances for 4
hands and feet. Bob Solem played the top (the easy)
part, and I played the bottom part and pedals. Anyway,
all went OK on the night, but there should have been
a bigger audience. Then we had Fauré's "Requiem"
jointly with Knox Choir on Palm Sunday. So that had
to be learned. Difficult stuff to play—lots of strange
harmonies, and, like the Liszt, constant changes of
tempi. But it's a most beautiful work. We also did
Fauré's "Psalm 84."

...Sorry about the "scratchy" letter—I still seem to be in a mental hubbub and all wound up. By the way, don't forget to let me know about the music for your wedding, and if you can, just a little information on the organ—number of stops, manuals, etc.; that's really all I need to know—I can judge from that what to play—I hope!

Much love to you both,
Nubbo

January 8, 1982.

Deat Mark,

Thank you so much for your letter and greetings. Over the past holidays I had no time to write, but now I wish you and your wife a "Happy Year 1982" in best healthy!

I habe been very busy,—just like your father wrote me from himself—with many Radio-Broadcastings and concerts. We made also with the choir a new record, and this new-one I send to the end of November for Christmas-gift to your father. But he never wrote some lines of acception? So I don't know, if he got this? If you write him some day, please ask him. May be, England has a better mail for Canada as we?

Enclosed, you find some Concert- and Radio-News. In the moment, I just heard the Canadian-Radio-News, and they said, there will be a graet Music-festival in some time in a Canadian town, but I couldn't heard in which-one, because it was just a noice round me.

Many greetings to you and Ann

Yours
L. Backes

28 When I was a teenager my father did much of his teaching at St. John's Cathedral—his students used the pipe organ in the church or the piano in the adjacent hall. Once a week he headed off to Cudworth, a small town about an hour's drive away; there he would teach the piano for six or seven hours at a stretch before getting into his car and driving back to Saskatoon. This can't have been fun, especially in winter.

But on Saturday mornings my father gave lessons at home, mostly to children from our neighbourhood. My bedroom was on the ground floor, next to the living room, and at 9 a.m. sharp I would be awakened by unpleasant noises from the piano. The first pupil of the day was a child whom my father began to call "Toad"—not to his face, of course. The boy had no talent for music, he seldom if ever practised, and week after week his scales and simple melodies showed no trace of improvement. It's hard to say what I found more annoying, the unpredictable and awkward silences or the wrong notes that followed. My father kept on teaching "Toad" because his mother, unlike some other parents, wrote a monthly cheque promptly and reliably. After my rude awakening, I would grab some breakfast in the kitchen and leave the house. The unhappy consequence, I now realize, was that I saw the weekly agonies of "Toad" as typical of my father's teaching.

He can't have been the best instructor for small and unmusical children. He didn't enter into their imaginative world, nor did he push his pupils to excel—though he was delighted when they pushed themselves. Organ students were a different matter. They were older; they already had some knowledge of the piano; and whatever their motives or ambitions, they were ready to play the instrument my father loved.

The student I remember my father mentioning with the greatest pleasure was a young man named Tom Packham. I knew him only slightly. Nearly forty years after leaving for Oxford, I googled his name out of curiosity. By then he was living in Winnipeg, having just retired as organist and choirmaster of the city's Anglican cathedral.

I wrote to Tom Packham and asked him about my father. And, as with my friend Tom Murison, I felt chastened by what he told me.

What a thrill to hear from you! Your wonderful father has been a constant presence for me through all these years of making music, both as educator and performer.

I approached him for organ lessons when I was a first-year student and eighteen years old. I had been exposed to the organ by my high-school music teacher, and had just been appointed organist and choirmaster of St. Timothy's Church. (Sounds grand, but they were broke and I was all they could afford.) This situation gave me access to not only the cozy little two-manual in my own church but also the organ in the cathedral. I recall with gratitude the generosity of your father in allowing me to practice for hours.

The main thing about him as a teacher was his tremendously encouraging approach. It was such a refreshing change from the intimidation of my piano teacher. He was so patient with me. He certainly did not have his eye on the clock—I was paying him for 45 minutes, and if I was ever there for an hour or an hour and a half, it was a quick lesson.

We had a very good time in the lessons. One of your dad's favourite expressions was "sorting through"—whether a Bach fugue or a trio sonata. Our conversations wandered too. He was a bit of a socialist. I remember him standing outside St. John's by his red Beetle, talking about politics. Finally he said, "I'm as red as this car"—and he got in and drove away.

My first real teaching job was in Spalding, which allowed me to keep in touch with your father since it was only 100 miles or so away. Harry graciously allowed me to continue singing in the cathedral choir whenever I was in Saskatoon for the weekend. I know now that your father's respectful and collegial approach to instruction helped me forge positive relationships with my own students. He personified an attitude my grandfather had tried hard to instill in me—he was proud to be English, but had no patience for any hint of arrogance or assumed superiority. If this quiet grace led to your father being underappreciated, he would never resort to self-promotion or bravado.

I saw this put to the test one evening when your parents came by for drinks with my parents and me. There was another couple there, friends of my parents, who thought they were being topical and clever talking about some of the pop organ-players of the '60s as if they were in any way peers of your father. Your father held his own in that ridiculous conversation in his usual gracious way. He impressed me—without being cruel, he put the other people in their place.

His "usual" gracious way? Was Tom Packham really talking about my father?

The organ is the most demanding of all instruments to play. You're controlling four extremities in addition to the tone colour and the registration. Just keeping track is a challenge. A melodic instrument only has one line to follow. Not to say that playing a flute or a violin is easy! But in a Bach fugue, you have to keep track of four or five lines. I can remember your father saying, "Always be aware of the lines—and that includes the inner voices."

As a performer, I've never heard anyone tackle the Romantics the way he did. We did some half-hour recitals at the cathedral in Saskatoon, and in one of them, your dad played the Prelude and Fugue on B.A.C.H. by Liszt. I don't know if I've heard anyone play it since—we all *own* a copy, of course. It's a long piece, and by the time you get to page 20 you're starting to feel there are too many notes. But your dad sat down and played it as if it were Happy Birthday.

Your father has been an invaluable role model to me. I'm an introvert, too, and we introverted people sometimes get shoved aside by the extroverted sorts. I have crossed paths with more celebrated organists, many of whom are hardly his equal in terms of actual playing. To me his real power was his personality.

My father's power lay in his personality: what had I missed all my life? What had I avoided seeing?

29 To play the organ well is to show fidelity to the work at hand. You don't perform Bach as if he were a heart-on-sleeve Romantic; you don't perform Liszt as if he were a pillar of the Enlightenment. To do so would be a distortion, an imposition. Your style, no matter how personal, is shaped by the nature of your material. This was a lesson I absorbed from my father, without quite realizing it, and took into my own work. Understand the structure. Trust the form. Listen to the inner voices.

My first love was poetry. But no one can make a living by writing poetry, and after I left Oxford I began to work as a freelance journalist. It was easier in the early 1980s to scratch a living by freelancing than it is today, and I was young—I was willing to scratch. A review, an interview, a profile, a radio script, an opinion piece, a backgrounder… On one occasion I sorted through the merits of the same anthology twice, damning it in *Books in Canada* but praising it in the *Times Literary Supplement*. If my inner voices were at risk of falling quiet, the outer one spoke loudly, and sometimes clearly. In those years I kept moving. I was hungry to explore new places, and with luck I could even get paid for it. Have pen, will travel.

The career I was forging was in prose. Yet poetry still held pride of place in my heart. From time to time, if a modest inspiration struck me, I would scribble down phrases on a used envelope or a scrap of notepaper, testing stray words and rhythms, altering the length of lines. Mealtimes might be delayed while I laboured to perfect a poem. But I never stuck a pencil behind an ear, and I made no connection between my father's work and my own. Had his fondness for wordplay affected my writing? At the time, I would have said, "No way."

In his letters my father commented on my articles, though he never said much about my poetry—not that I ever told him much. But he was delighted to hear about the places where I'd travelled. Through me, I now realize, he was able to appease a little of his wanderlust.

Occasionally—visiting a friend in St. Andrew's, for instance—I would recall a fragment of childhood. My father was not a golfer; I would never become a golfer. The presence of the Royal and Ancient Golf Club on the wind-blown coast of Fife meant less to me than it does to many Canadians. But as a boy in Lethbridge, I had often sat beside my father on our living-room sofa, watching *Shell's Wonderful World of Golf.* The program was broadcast on Sunday afternoon, and by then we would have completed our walk around Henderson Lake. My mother would feed us tea and cookies. Each week the gaudy music introduced a city somewhere older and more glamorous than Lethbridge. Courtesy of Shell, we could dream about the wider world: anywhere, but somewhere else.

My father had little interest in professional golf, and absolutely no interest in the promotional messages from Shell. Refinement, in his mind, had nothing to do with refineries. But despite the limitations of a small black-and-white TV set, he devoured the travelogue segments of the show with a hungry longing. Delhi, Athens, Barcelona, Singapore: he had never seen such places. He would never see such places. I would see them all.

Our bungalow on Corvette Crescent in Lethbridge was thousands of miles away from the bungalow on Offa's Road in Knighton. My father had come a long way, but he wanted to go even further. I sensed his desire and pulled it inward, making it part of myself.

30 "All musical people seem to me happy," the English wit Sydney Smith once wrote; "it is the most engrossing pursuit; almost the only innocent and unpunished passion." Punishment was on its way, however. In 1983 Annie and I embarked on a rickety Polish ship and sailed from England to make a new life in Montreal.

31 Until I began to write this book I had succeeded in forgetting that I urged my parents to move to Montreal. Somehow I'd convinced myself that it was my mother's idea. Perhaps it was—as a boy, I had grown expert at intuiting her every wish—but the evidence of letters is clear. I can imagine what I was feeling, though I have no idea what I was thinking.

June 1, 1984.

Dear Mark and Annie,

...It has been the worst spring we can remember over here. All of which seems to indicate to us MOVE. Thank you for your long letter, Mark; we think your suggestions about moving from Saskatoon are good. When one gets away from here one realises how much out in the sticks we are here—culturally that is. We much appreciated your remarks and suggestions, and we think that a move to Montreal would be a good thing.

...I was away during most of the Festival performances here, at North Battleford, disappointing numerous people there, poor things! However, they might as well get used to disappointments early—it helps for later on. Actually I enjoyed the time up there, although it was busy and hard-packed, festivals always are. The only thing was that the hotel food was terrible, otherwise no complaints.

Must end, Mum will be waiting, we want to post to you straight away.

Lots of love to you both,

The letter was unsigned. Below it, on the same thin blue sheet of paper, my mother added some handwritten lines.

Hi, VERY dear Mark and Annie,

What a marvellous letter! Thank you so much & especially for your loving concern. Do you suppose there will be a chance of accomplishing the move in October? The thought of another winter here is a sort of back-of-the-mind dread. I am sure Bunny should be doing less—considerably less—but if he gives up

All Saints he would be giving up the rewarding &
enjoyable choir, small in numbers though it is, and
if he gives up 3rd Ave. he would lose the worthwhile
organ, apart, in either case, from the hurt feelings of
one church when the other was retained. Anyway, you
can see how greatly we appreciate your suggestion. We
wouldn't want to be under your feet or in any way
a burden, but it would be wonderful to be near you
instead of 2,000 miles away.

…Much, much love to you both,
M.

Both my parents had suffered bouts of illness in the
early 1980s. Nothing serious, as it turned out, but it felt
like a wake-up call. My parents' marriage had always been
one in which my father initiated any significant change.
Now, for once, my mother began to take the lead. She
worried about my father's heavy workload, perhaps not
realizing how deeply it sustained him. She was approaching
seventy and she hoped for a grandchild. Over the phone,
we discussed the idea of a move.

My father went along with the idea. I assume he felt he
owed her this; I didn't ask too closely. Annie and I began
to make inquiries among the churches of English-speaking Montreal. We knew my father could never survive

without a pipe organ at his disposal. Two possibilities came to nothing, but the third—the Church of the Advent, a small Anglo-Catholic parish in lower Westmount—offered him a job.

Once the domain of wealthy families who owned mansions up the hill, the Advent had become a haven for immigrants and refugees. The parish priest, in my parents' initial years there, was a grey-haired Irishman with a dry wit and a love of classical music. What could be better? I thought. If my father wanted to add traditional British items like "The Coventry Carol" or "The Holly and the Ivy" to the choir's repertoire, he would meet no opposition.

The move took longer to arrange than my mother had wished, but in the summer of 1985 my parents packed up their belongings once again. Because of the timing, they cancelled a recital tour in Germany. My mother sent a postcard shortly before their flight from Saskatoon to Montreal, thanking Annie and me for phoning twice within a few days. "It was very good for Bunny: his morale was slipping and today, going into town, he observed that this should have been the day of the first of the concerts in Germany. Now, after your call, he is feeling better." He almost succeeded, nonetheless, in missing the plane.

Many years later, when my widowed mother had been diagnosed with vascular dementia, I wrote to her old friends in Saskatoon to give them the news. One of them replied: "We both sang in All Saints under the direction of your wonderful father and so we have happy memories of him. We still have a tape recording of your father's composition for the mass in the Book of Alternative Services which he played on our piano while waiting for his plane departure from Saskatoon. We had such a good time singing and discussing it that he nearly missed his flight entirely. It was held for him and he did an excellent job of running full throttle." By then my father was sixty-eight. I don't believe there was a minute in the remaining nine years of his life when he was happy to have run so fast.

My mother loved Montreal from the start. She was undaunted by its mix of cultures and languages. She enrolled in a French course. She made new friends.

My father hated the place. The Church of the Advent had a sweet-toned organ, but it was a modest instrument with only two manuals and a dozen or so stops. The choir was small, and not everyone in it could sing. My father had come to be regarded as one of the leading organists in the Prairie provinces; now he felt like a nobody again. With his poor ear for languages, he did not attempt to learn French. His enjoyment at attending organ recitals in the vast churches of Montreal was tempered by a sour awareness that he would never have the chance to perform there. In Saskatoon he had a few dozen students, some of them talented; in Montreal he had no students at all. My mother wrote out a few advertisements by hand, and placed them on the bulletin boards of corner stores and cafes along Monkland and Sherbrooke Streets, but nobody took up the offer. Wary of being pulled into the vortex of my father's needs, Annie and I did not join the Church of the Advent. He had the dignity not to ask.

My parents' latest car, a Rabbit, had been sent to Montreal by train. When it arrived, my father faced a daily nightmare of driving and parking in a fast-paced metropolis full of potholes, roadworks, one-way streets, and confusing signs in a foreign tongue. For a few months he kept a Saskatchewan licence plate on the front of the car and a Quebec plate on the rear—a gesture of divided loyalties that earned him a fine from the Montreal police. Aggrieved, he sold the Rabbit and relied on public transport. He held on to his old licence plate, three green letters and three green numbers displayed against a white background, with some sheaves of wheat in the middle. I found it after his death, filed away among his concert programs and the scores of his final compositions.

In 1986, thanks to Lotte Backes, he again played several concerts in Germany—a newspaper review of one recital, in the southwestern state of Baden-Württemberg, has a headline that reads, in translation, "Masterly virtuosity." The concert took place on the evening of my mother's seventieth birthday. My father was delighted to be back in the country where pipe organs had reached the height of their influence and esteem. As he knew, the suns, stars, and angels that adorned many of the German organs built in J.S. Bach's era were symbols of heaven—to hear one being played, or to contemplate it in silence, was to gain a taste of heaven on Earth. A Nuremberg organist named Johann Erasmus Kindermann had even turned sacred music into the Holy Trinity, or vice versa. God the Father, he wrote in 1655, "is the Capellmeister, or leader, of all the choirs of musicians." God the Son "leads from the basso continuo as the organist of heaven with everlasting joy and blessedness. He plays on the pedals with his feet and all his enemies stumble." (God the Holy Spirit seems a bit of a letdown—merely "the sweet, gentle, and blessed wind who dries our tears.") If Britain would always be the home of my father's emotions, Germany had come to feel like his artistic home.

But the adrenalin that flowed in him abroad could not make up for what he felt as rejection and humiliation in Montreal. The leading organists of the city ignored him. He wrote four short waltzes for piano: they were never performed. And in 1987 came a particularly harsh blow. Lotte Backes delivered it with her usual directness.

Dear Mr. Abley and Mary,

We have no more the good musik-situation as we had before and I must write you a disillusion. One of the organists from the see wrote me, that he cant take no more organists from me because they have so much joung organists in the country, and they want to play first. And here in Bln is the situation no more as formerly, I have more choir-concerts, and brass. The Radio has also changed his Program, after the News they bring pop-music from the jongsters, and this is so primitiv, that we turn of.

Is not also a Manager for you in your town?

No, there was no manager. And there would be no more concerts in Germany.

Age did not make my father rest on his laurels; it made him all the more conscious of the laurels he had never received, and the ones he had discarded. In 1988 Eric Burt wrote another article about him for the *Star-Phoenix*—a Saskatchewan music company had just published the setting of the Anglican liturgy that almost made him miss his flight to Montreal—and in it, my father declared: "Canada is my country and Saskatoon is my city." Wishful thinking—by then he had been a resident of Montreal for three years. I don't believe he'd ever really thought of Saskatoon as the sticks; but if he had, he was longing to be back in the midst of them.

He had also become a grandfather. Kate survived her terrible birth, fifteen weeks too early, but it soon became clear that her eyesight and breathing were less than adequate; she was prone to infections. My mother threw herself into her new identity—"Granny"—with confidence and delight. My father handled Kate as if he had seldom held a baby before. Having been displaced once in his wife's affections, he now found himself displaced all over again.

He loved Kate, and set a Dylan Thomas poem to music for her: "The moon is your lady, she sings you to sleep; / The stars are the dew on her hair…" Yet he refused to be defined by grandfatherhood. It was an unmusical role for him to play. Besides, he was developing a new grudge in life. To his longstanding prejudices against Americans and Jews, he added a new one: French Canadians. Mildly sympathetic toward Quebec when he lived in Western Canada, he changed his tune once he arrived in a province where French-speakers are in the majority. A few diehards at the Church of the Advent told him that Quebec was trampling the rights of English-speakers, and he was ready to believe them. His recitals began to feature more music by British composers.

Those were years of high political tension, and when the Oka crisis erupted near Montreal in July 1990, it was clear where my father's sympathies lay. He wrote a short tone poem for piano, "The Pines of Oka," a musical impression of the events of that summer. "The music is constructed basically on a four-note leitmotiv," he explained in a prefatory note. "The opening and closing pages portray the calm and peace of the forest, which are broken by the confrontation.... The piece is dedicated to the people of the Mohawk Nation, with admiration and respect." Compared to the Québécois, the Mohawks were underdogs. On his behalf I sent the score to a Mohawk cultural centre, but there was never any reply.

32 A few years before his death, my father experienced an intense and terrifying headache. It lasted for two or three days. The headache skewed his visual perception in odd ways: he could read the words of a newspaper article but fail to understand the headline; he could clearly see sideways, but not straight ahead. A doctor at the Montreal Neurological Hospital realized the symptoms were those of a stroke, and prescribed a new drug in the hope of preventing a recurrence. The drug did its job and more: not only did my father's perceptions return to normal, he never endured another migraine.

Yet he remained as sullen as ever. Indeed, he was now a very grumpy old man. The fury of helplessness made him desperate. A few weeks after his stroke, I asked him how his appetite was. "Fine," he snapped. "Why shouldn't it be?"

No reason, Dad, no reason.

By then I had come to believe he should undergo an intensive course of psychotherapy. "If only he could let his feelings out," I thought, "instead of allowing them to fester inside." For eighteen months I had seen a psychiatrist every week, and it did me a power of good. Yet the family dynamics were so convoluted that I never told my father about my own anxieties, my own therapy, my efforts at healing. I wouldn't have minded him knowing. But he would have passed on the news to my mother, and I felt unable to cope with her inquisitive sympathy, her puzzled distress, her reproachful guilt.

I sat outside on the balcony of his apartment on a warm afternoon—my wife, daughter, and mother were all inside—and told him that I thought he should see a therapist.

"I can find you a good one," I said. "All the costs will be covered by the Quebec medical plan. You won't have to pay a cent. I know you've been feeling unhappy and I think this could be really helpful." I paused. "It's nothing to be ashamed of, you know."

He looked at me and said nothing. I looked at him and said nothing. He looked away and said nothing. I looked away and said nothing. He went on saying nothing. I went on saying nothing. And he outlasted me: unable to stand the tension, I invented an excuse to go back inside. A few minutes later, he followed. Neither of us alluded to this again.

By then my father was hunting for work elsewhere. My parents subscribed to the *Church Times*, the leading Anglican weekly in Britain, and one day my mother confided to me that he had begun mailing out inquiry letters in response to job ads for organists. Her dismay was diluted by guilt that she had, as she believed, dragged my father to a city where he would always be miserable. Now she felt unable to protest. I was dismayed too, but I wasn't particularly worried—I couldn't believe anyone in their right mind would hire a seventy-three-year-old organist, sight unseen, sound unheard, living across the Atlantic.

Wrong again. After writing letters that earned a negative response, or none at all, my father applied to be the organist and choirmaster of a church in Barnsley, a coal-mining town in North Yorkshire best known as the home of Arthur Scargill, the firebrand head of the National Union of Mineworkers. By 1991 all but one of Barnsley's mines had closed. In the past it had been a centre for the linen, wire-making, and glass-blowing trades—all of which were now in trouble too. The town's employment rate was low, its per capita income half the national average. Barnsley has a particular type of lamb chop, a football team even less successful than Swindon Town, and a profusion of brass bands. Its musical traditions involve cornets and tubas, not church choirs. Maybe nobody except my father would have dreamed of moving there to work as an organist. At any rate, his application was successful.

My parents had never set foot in Barnsley. That didn't stop them. The job paid poorly and came with no accommodation. That didn't stop them. Until the age of eighty, neither of them would be entitled to a British pension. That didn't stop them. Kate was three years old. That didn't stop them.

I didn't stop them either.

33

Two pictures. Two moments. Two men. No, one man.

My father is perched on the organ bench of St. John's Cathedral in Saskatoon, turned slightly away from the manuals so that a photographer can capture his face at a flattering angle. His hands rest on his thighs, fingers spread out, ready to take up the challenge of the sheet music in the top left corner of the picture. There's no sign of his cassock, surplice, or hood, for no service is in progress. Instead he wears a dark blazer, a white shirt, and a college tie. The tie, like the large crest on his blazer, suggests an urge to display his qualifications: he had diplomas from three of London's music colleges. If anybody doubted him, he could point to the string of initials stretching out after his name: ARCM, FTCL, FLCM…Few people knew what all these capital letters stood for, but they made a point— especially for a man who could not use simpler initials like BA.

He's posing at a three-manual organ, the standard size in large Canadian churches. This particular model is the work of an English firm named Hill, Norman and Beard. When it was installed here in 1957, it joined other bits and pieces of "the Old Country": stones from Glastonbury Abbey and Exeter Cathedral, a cross from Canterbury. The pulpit and altar were made in simulated marble by the Doulton company of Staffordshire, and the whole building embodies the Gothic Revival style so popular in Victorian Britain. But one glance at the exterior of St. John's Cathedral would be enough to tell anyone this is no English building. The church has the colour of the Red Fort in Delhi—almost shockingly bright, as though to amaze the South Saskatchewan River across the road. Inside the walls of Prairie brick and terra cotta, the organ is a stylish, sweet-voiced instrument, so long as it's not misbehaving. Like my father, it has moods. When its caprices finally become too much for the city's Anglicans to bear, the instrument will be dismantled, packed up, and shipped off to a small church in northern Canada, eventually to die by fire.

My father looks comfortable in front of the three keyboards. He is smiling, showing a few teeth, not quite catching the photographer's eye: he prefers not to look directly at the camera. Light beams down onto the organ, glinting off my father's right eye, his forehead, the tip of his nose. Not far from his face, the ranks of stops begin: an 8-foot trumpet, the 16-foot sub-bass, a 32-foot resultant bass (you have to be careful using that one)…The pedalboard is out of view. But my father seems to fit the space. He sits at the console like a man at ease, someone in the midst of a good journey.

Which perhaps he was. His face has an ageless quality, as though, once he sat down to perform, years of stress and anxiety would fall away into the shadows of the cathedral, to be gathered up and worn again when he left the console behind. It's not a conventionally handsome face but there is beauty in it, the relaxed beauty of a man who loves his work. His face is only lightly creased, his receding hair not entirely grey. Bushy silver sideburns, roaming down toward the base of his ears, help fix this moment in time: the mid-1970s, when my father was not quite sixty years old.

The picture was taken by a photographer from the *Saskatoon Star-Phoenix*. It would illustrate a feature article published under the headline "Triumphs dot Abley career."

A picture, all told, of a father any son could be proud of. A picture the organist would use for his own purposes. Five years after it appeared in the newspaper, this photograph would take up most of the front page of his new publicity brochure. "HENRY ABLEY, *Concert Organist*": this was an image he liked to present to the world. The photograph suited his ambitions. It helped relieve his fears.

The second picture is harder to describe. My father seldom drew—drawing was among the innumerable skills he was convinced he lacked. But from the age of two, it was Kate's great pleasure and consolation. One day, when Annie and I were at work and my parents were looking after her, she must have asked my father to draw her a picture. Given an oversized sheet of glossy paper and a box of Crayolas, he produced some impromptu portraits of the family.

Cartoon drawings, really. Little more than coloured stick figures. Stick figures with a story to tell.

The figure who takes up the most space is me. I am outlined in mauve, standing with a big sloppy grin on my face, my right hand lifted high. My torso is a plump shield, wider than I would like. There's no sign of a beard, but my father has generously given me lots of hair.

Beside me, across the top of the page, are my family's two pets. Freya, sketched in brown, is recognizably a cat, but Fergus, drawn in purple, resembles a sausage with four feet and a tail. His grinning, humanoid face appears to be topped by a pair of horns. Not that I mean to sneer; it's hard for any amateur to make a decent likeness of an overweight white cat. The cats and I are plumper than any of the four people in the bottom row.

To the left stands Annie, looking surprised in green. Her mouth is a mere dot. My mother comes next, dark blue except for a sleeveless orange dress. She is smiling; her eyebrows are raised; nothing in the drawing suggests that she is well over seventy years old. Kate is at the bottom right, sketched in purple like one of the cats. My father hasn't included her glasses. She too has a smile.

The remaining figure on the page is my father's self-portrait, the only one I know. He stands between his wife and granddaughter, outlined dramatically in black: there is no other black ink on the page. He is marginally shorter than Kate, who in all likelihood was then between two and four years old. His body looks emaciated—a quarter inch wide on the page, it could easily fit inside mine. The trio of wispy hairs that rise from his scalp are matched by three horizontal lines running across his forehead. His eyebrows slope down towards the middle of his face at a forty-five-degree angle. His ears stick out, and his eyes are scrunched together near a spot that must signify a nose. But the most prominent feature is his mouth. It points down sharply, the shape of an inverted "V."

When he drew this picture, my father could not have been in one of his blue moods, his brown studies, his black depths. In his most depressed hours or days, he would never have mustered the energy to pick up a box of crayons and draw a picture for his grandchild. Most of the figures on the page look cheerful, and so is his energetic attempt at a street scene on the reverse side of the page: a house, a car, a few trees and red flowers, a bird the size of a passing cyclist.

I imagine it gave my father a sharp and angry pleasure to compose this self-portrait. Grotesque though it may be, the picture is a faithful rendering of what, after years in Montreal, he felt his life had become. I can imagine a newspaper headline: "Failures dot Abley career." Diminutive, ugly, tense; defeated; powerless. No one else would have described him that way. But that's how he saw himself.

There is a selfishness to the portrait—the self-absorption of my father's long depression, one that could render even the desires of a vulnerable grandchild subservient to the all-consuming saga of himself. I'm sure my father loved his family. But love can't always overcome despair.

ME! MOI! MIR!

34 I don't know if he drew that picture before or after the move to Barnsley. "To live, you must risk calamity," a pianist remarks in Kim Echlin's *Under the Visible Life*, one of the finest novels about music that I know. "Abandon old ways to create something new. Love the life under the visible life." My father had made up his mind to create something new; he was determined to take a risk. Calamity, for him, was the definition of life in Montreal.

Should I have tried to stop him? I've asked myself that question countless times, and I still don't know the answer. By 1991 I was tired of looking out for my father—I had been doing this for decades. I was angry that he would uproot himself again: it seemed like an admission of failure, even a betrayal. Had I failed too? I was also sick at heart for my mother. After I drove the two of them to Mirabel Airport on a chilly afternoon in March, I climbed up a flight of stairs to a viewing gallery that overlooked a section of the departures area. My parents were still in sight, unsure where to turn. My mother looked desperate. The previous evening, for the first and only time in her life, she had sobbed in Annie's arms.

My parents had bought expensive tickets that gave them an option to return to Montreal on any open date within the next twelve months. The cost of the airfare and the furniture shipment to England exhausted most of their paltry savings. I half-expected them to creep back in a little under a year.

But I couldn't just let them go. Like so many only children, I suffered from an overdeveloped sense of duty. And now responsibility had become intertwined with guilt. In those years I was working full-time for the *Montreal Gazette*, and the contract allowed me a week off in the winter. Instead of travelling somewhere warm with my wife and child, or staying home to give Annie a much-needed break, I booked a short trip to England, the departure date falling about ten days after my parents had left. I thought I could help them settle into Barnsley. Lifting, carrying, phoning, shopping, driving, cleaning, making inquiries on their behalf: there must be some practical help I could give. I also suspected my mother would need many hugs.

At first there was no word. Then, a few days before my flight, I picked up the phone and heard her voice on the end of the line.

"Are you calling from your new home?" I said.

"No, dear, I'm calling from Walsall."

Walsall is a town in the West Midlands, effectively a suburb of Birmingham. It's nowhere near Barnsley. My mother sounded both exhausted and relieved.

"Walsall? What are you doing there?"

"We're staying with Joyce. Things didn't—work out in Barnsley." A long pause. "Can you come and see us here?"

So I flew to London, caught a train to Birmingham, and spent part of my winter break staying with a friend of my mother from teachers' college, a widow with a large enough house to accommodate all three of us with ease. My father was battered but undaunted—he'd had an adventure. He'd tried to create something new. I went for a walk with him in a windswept park, early kites careening above our heads, a few children racing past us, their voices clear and joyful. True, he said, the rooming house in Barnsley had been a disaster. True, there weren't any decent flats to rent. True, the rector had proved unwelcoming. But he didn't want to dwell on all that. Barnsley was a fascinating town. He was happy to have discovered it. Did I know about its history in the British labour movement?

No, and I didn't want to know. I couldn't care less about the British labour movement. As far as I was concerned, the entire population of Barnsley could hurl itself and its fascinating history into an abandoned coal mine. What I wanted was a mouthful of remorse.

What I wanted was some recognition of the pain he'd put my family through in the preceding months. What I wanted was some trace of acknowledgement that the whole attempt to settle in Barnsley had been a horrible mistake. And I didn't get it. Instead my parents flew back to Montreal after an absence of two weeks—their fourth time emigrating from Britain to Canada—and my father got rehired at the Church of the Advent, which had delayed choosing his replacement. But as they had given up their Montreal apartment, and as most of their belongings were now somewhere on the St. Lawrence River or the Atlantic Ocean, slowly sailing off in the wrong direction, my parents would spend the next few months living out of suitcases and sleeping on couches in our basement. My mother was overjoyed to spend so much time with Kate. My father played the little organ and conducted the little choir.

The experience took its toll on everyone. When my parents were out of our house at last, Annie and I enjoyed an overwhelming sense of relief. I also felt enormous guilt at having put her through all this, as if at the age of thirty-six I had betrayed my own family and displayed a glaring failure to grow up.

The relief, the sense of freedom, didn't last for long. Soon after my parents moved into their new apartment, my mother fell ill. She would spend five weeks in hospital with what was eventually diagnosed as an infection of the heart valve, its origin unknown, its treatment challenging. At first the illness did not respond to antibiotics, and my mother's body weakened. I faced the bleak prospect of coping with my father as a widower. One day I went round to their home to see how he was faring, and discovered that he didn't know where to find the can opener.

Montreal had accepted him back. Yet he went on looking for an escape. An ad in the *Church Times* announced that the parish church in Fowey had a vacancy for an organist again. Fourteen years had now passed since my parents left Fowey for Saskatoon. Regardless of his age, regardless of the health or needs of his wife, regardless of his lack of savings—and forgetful of his previous rheumatism—he fired off a letter of application. He wanted to emigrate *again*. Dylan Thomas might have approved: my father was refusing to go gentle into that good night. But was there a vestige of sanity in this rage against the dying of the light? The church in Fowey had enough wisdom, or enough other applicants, to say no.

My mother recovered from the heart infection, finally, and lived for two more decades. As for my father, in the fall of 1992 he began to suffer some unpleasant intestinal symptoms. He underwent a barium x-ray, a colonoscopy, a biopsy. He played a December concert regardless. On Christmas Eve, he learned that he was suffering from colon cancer. The Christmas services went off without a hitch.

35 After Christmas I phoned a friend whose father had died of colon cancer. "All we got was jargon," he said. "They can spin the jargon all around you. If the news is bad, nobody wants to deliver it. They'll do all they can to avoid bad news." My friend added, "They put my father through radiation and all these other procedures although they knew from the start there was no hope."

The next year is a long blur. When my father was diagnosed with cancer, Annie was pregnant with our second child, and in March 1993 Megan was born. She was a spirited baby. By then my father had been operated on.

Cancer

The white coat was pressed and terse:
faced with its verdict
my father straightened his suit,

his blood-linen tie, his best shoes,
and on the appointed day,
leaving nothing disorderly,

caught the bus to Admissions,
observing each block slip
away, the long roads of the city

where his greatest pleasure
was mordant complaint
growing, car by car, invisible

as though a distant trumpet
had called, and his cells alone
were free to answer.

The tumour turned out to be Stage C, the cancer having spread into three lymph nodes. Bad news. The sur-
geon told me, almost as an aside, and without stopping
to explain the implications, "We took out the area in the
prostate that was involved." My father remained in hospital
for ten days. Near the end of his stay, a radiation oncologist
swept into his room, announced the scheduled treatments,
and left without answering questions.

My father endured a week of chemotherapy in March,
another in early April. On St. George's Day, April 23, he

performed a concert at the Church of the Advent. It was devoted entirely to music by English composers. If he was now going down, he meant to go down in flames.

The ensuing radiation was a trial, and my father did not complain. In August and September he had further sessions of chemotherapy, and he didn't complain on those occasions either. If something had to be done, it had to be done. He continued to play the organ every Sunday, and gave a pre-Christmas concert. Aside from performing music by the usual suspects, himself included, he wasn't about to let the year vanish without marking the possible 450th anniversary of William Byrd's birth and the undisputed 100th anniversary of Peter Tchaikovsky's death.

"How do you think he's doing?" my mother whispered in between two of the pieces.

"Wonderfully," I said.

"He's had a lot of grief."

"*What?*"

"Not being able to use the pistons."

He let out the larger pain, so to speak, in dark comments addressed to my mother, and sometimes to me as well.

"I'm stuck here for life," he said one day.

Part of me felt like answering, "Suck it up, Dad!" I didn't, of course. I was still too polite, and besides, like my mother, I was now at the permanent mercy of his morale.

My father had been put through what the doctors called "a full curative dose of radiation." It proved useless. In the spring of 1994 his cancer came raging back. In June he underwent a second operation, this one requiring a colostomy. The physical indignity was made worse by the knowledge that he had not, in fact, beaten the odds. He had always been a fastidious man as well as a grumbler. But now that he could no longer be fastidious, he declined to grumble. He took his sickness like a man—an interesting phrase, I found myself thinking.

A few months later he went for x-rays to learn if the cancer had spread. This time, for reasons that escape me, I was the first in the family to hear the news and deliver the results. Perhaps his doctor was away at the time, and rather than have a stranger inform my father, I was drafted in. Perhaps the idea was to spare my mother's feelings. Or perhaps, as my friend had warned me, doctors prefer not to engage in the kind of conversation I was about to have— the kind of speech I was about to give.

On a bright, warm morning in late September I knocked on the door of my parents' apartment. The exhausting humidity of the Montreal summer was over at last. My parents were sitting together on the sofa. I noticed how small they looked.

"Well, the doctors told me the x-ray results," I said. "And the cancer has spread a long way. It's in your liver,

Dad. It's in your lungs as well. They won't do any more active treatment. They said it's a matter of palliative care—keeping the pain under control, and making sure you don't suffer too much.

"No, they didn't give me a timeline. They never do. But they said someone from the hospital will be contacting you soon."

My parents met the news with quiet dignity. I don't recall their exact words—neither of them had much to say. I left them side by side on the sofa, holding hands. From the sidewalk below, as I unlocked my car, I looked up at the window of their apartment: neither of them waved me off. I drove to the *Gazette* newsroom to put in a day's work.

What I remember with appalled clarity is how I felt. There was a degree of sadness, of course. I was anxious about the pain my father might endure. But with another part of my mind, I was relieved, even exultant. *He'll be gone within a few months*, I thought. *He's finally going to die!*

I had been waiting for this moment for years.

36 He made a special effort for Thanksgiving. I drove my parents out to my house in the suburbs, where Annie had cooked a magnificent turkey. My father played a little with Kate and Megan. I took a picture of him trying manfully to smile. A few days later, in my parents' apartment, I reminisced with him. I mentioned the many concerts he'd played in Germany over the years, and the few occasions I'd been there at his side.

My father nodded. "Good times," he said. "It's what it's all about."

Good times? I was amazed. Such a banal phrase. Such a vital phrase. A phrase I had never associated with my father.

The disease soon began to attack his mind. One evening my mother phoned and asked if I could attend the Church of the Advent on Sunday; this might, she thought, be his last time at the organ. The service would take place on October 30, the day before Halloween: in both the

Christian and the pagan calendar, a time for remembering the dead. Montreal's streets were full of jack-o'-lanterns. Plastic ghosts fluttered from branches.

I arrived at the church to find a scattering of people in the pews, a server lighting candles on the altar, and my mother in a state of barely concealed panic. Normally she would be kneeling, her eyes closed in prayer, or else she would be gazing in reverence at the decorative altarpiece: Jesus and a flock of angels, painted against a sky crammed with stars. Now she was sitting bolt upright, having trouble keeping still.

Robert Warren, the recently appointed rector, walked down a side aisle to greet me. A smart and burly man on the threshold of middle age, he came straight to the point.

"Can you stay with him at the organ? He's going to need some help."

I had sat beside my mother near the front of many churches through hundreds of hours of worship. Never before had I spent a service at the organ, beside my father.

I walked up the chancel steps to the console. My father was already there. He said a brief hello in a distracted manner—the concentration required to prepare his music was using up all of his energy. Above the organ was a stained-glass window of St. George killing a green-scaled dragon.

"Can I do anything to help?" I asked.

"I'll be all right," he said.

Soon it was time for the first piece, a choral prelude by Bach with the English name "Lord Jesus Christ, Be Present Now." My father found the piece amid a large pile of papers, and I helped him arrange the score on the music stand above the two manuals. Then he began to play. His hands were quivering and the notes sounded watery, nothing like the rich and mellow tones of his usual style. But he got through the prelude safely.

Father Warren emerged then from the vestry and in his big, confident voice announced the processional hymn: "Thee will I love, my strength, my tower." My father had chosen it, as well as all the other hymns that would be sung that morning. The Advent had not been a wealthy parish for decades, and within a few years it would close its doors for good; a small sign of its poverty was that it had never replaced the 1938 *Book of Common Praise* with a more recent alternative, so that many of the hymnbooks were on the verge of falling apart. But the worshippers stood up and found the hymn as if nothing was amiss.

To begin with, their faith seemed justified. My father laid out the familiar tune, and a modest procession began a slow voyage around the church: the priest, three servers, a lay reader, and a red-robed choir of five. The choir included an elderly lady who could no longer sing and a younger woman who could seldom keep a tune. Anthems were a thing of the past. The procession passed a side altar, where the small blue light of the Blessed Sacrament burned with a constant flame, and kept on going.

In the second verse my father lost his place. "I thank thee, who hast overthrown / My foes, and healed my wounded mind"—here the organ slowed and fell silent. My father stared at the score. I couldn't see the reaction of the priest and choir, who had reached the back of the building. There was a brief agonizing wait. Silence filled the church. At last my father went back to the beginning of the melody, and the choir fumbled into the third verse.

Father Warren glanced at me when he stepped up to the main altar. I could see the anxiety in his eyes. Usually his opening prayers would be followed by "Kyrie Eleison"— Lord, have mercy—chanted by the choir and congregation with an organ accompaniment. On that day, as so often, the music was to be the simple setting for the *Book of Alternative Services* that my father had composed in his final weeks in Saskatoon. It was ideal for small congregations: they would sing in unison, with the organ supporting and encouraging their voices. Now my father searched for the score amid his heap of papers. Not only had he written it, he had played it dozens of times—surely he knew it by heart. I hesitated, wanting to help, not wanting to make things worse by inter-ference. "The Mass book," he hissed at me. "Where is it?"

I had no idea. What did it look like? Seconds ticked by, and Father Warren made an executive decision. "This morning," he announced, "we will *say* the Kyrie." I turned to my father, nervous even now of some fit of bitter pique. But he showed no anger. He just sat on the organ bench: silent, motionless, helpless. High above the instrument the dragon writhed, speared through the mouth.

The congregation went on to recite "Gloria in Excelsis," a much longer text than the Kyrie. They did the same with a psalm and the Creed. It was as if all my father's music had evaporated into thin air. But it's hard to recite a hymn. One was coming up, just before the gospel. And now my father had found the right page in the right book. He played the hymn—"Blest are the pure in heart"—without a hitch.

The sermon gave my father a chance to relax. He did not close his eyes. Nor did he look my way. After the sermon Father Warren said a special prayer for a member of the choir, a refugee from the Seychelles who had been a victim of domestic violence and had entered Canada illegally; now she and her two children faced deportation. I could see the woman fighting back tears. The priest went on to tell God the names of sick or disabled people for whom special prayers had been asked. At the end, in a low voice, he added: "And for Harry."

Perhaps the prayer had an immediate effect. The words of the offertory hymn, "At the name of Jesus," had been set to festive music by Ralph Vaughan Williams, and my father got through it without incident. There would be three more chants before the communion—a Sanctus, a Benedictus, and an Agnus Dei—and I expected these to be said, like the Kyrie and the Gloria. But no, my father had found his Mass book at last, and when the proper moment arrived for each of the chants, he began to play its melody—*his* melody. The church was fragrant now with a blend of candle wax, altar flowers, and incense. Heads in the pews were bowed low.

I helped my father to the altar rail to make his communion. To my mother, a firm believer in the doctrine of "the real presence," this wafer of unleavened bread was more than just a symbol of salvation: Father Warren's prayer of consecration had transformed it into the body of Christ. I don't know what my father thought about that. He held the bread in the palm of his hand for a long time, looking at it, seemingly unsure what to do with it, before raising it to his mouth. Then he took a sip of wine.

It gave him strength. For after he had received communion he went back to the organ and began to play a tranquil hymn for the small choir to sing. When it ended, my father improvised for a minute or two on the melody, "Lord, enthroned in heavenly splendour." His fingers still had music in them. I could close my eyes, listen to the organ, and almost forget he was dying.

The day's final hymn, "King of glory, king of peace," was a setting of a poem by a great Welsh author. George

Herbert had been born in Montgomery, a small town in the hill country north of Knighton. Two centuries after his death, the poem gained a new life in the form of a musical setting by another Welshman, an impoverished composer and music teacher named Joseph David Jones. This would be the last hymn my father would play.

> Thou hast granted my request,
> thou hast heard me;
> thou didst note my working breast,
> thou hast spared me...

And he played it well. Standing beside the console, I felt enormous relief as the final chord rang out. My father had been heard, he had been noted. For the moment, perhaps he had been spared.

Relief vanished in a flash. My father was searching for the postlude, another choral prelude by Bach. Seconds ticked away in silence. A piece of sheet music dropped to the floor by the pedalboard. I bent down and picked it up; it was not the one he wanted. He couldn't find the right score, and I didn't know where to look. A teen-aged server walked back up the aisle carrying a long candle-snuffer, and peered our way with sad curiosity. Finally my father gave up searching and played the prelude again.

"Music in church," he had written in Sault Ste. Marie half a lifetime earlier, "is designed in the first place for the glory of God. J.S. Bach, greatest of church musicians, had the habit of writing at the end of his completed compositions 'Solo Dei Gloria'—'To the glory of God alone'—and if that devotion and humility can be practised constantly, then the second purpose, to edify the worshipper, will follow."

Lord Jesus Christ, be present now. Solo Dei Gloria. My father swung his feet off the pedalboard and looked at me, his eyes hollow with fatigue and grief.

37 As the last leaves fell from the most stubborn maples, cancer tore through my father's pelvis, his liver, his lungs, his digestive tract. He had been taking 15 milligrams of morphine twice a day. The dose was now too low, and the doctors doubled the hit. This reduced his pain at the price of clouding his mind.

A few days after his last service at the Church of the Advent, my mother and I brought him a "living will." Its aim was to prevent medical staff from using what are euphemistically called "heroic measures"—the kind of high-tech intervention that forestalls death, regardless of the wishes or sufferings of the patient. The living will could take effect only if my father, when he signed it, was in full possession of his faculties. He read through the document and seemed to understand it. But at the place where he was meant to sign, he wrote a final variant of his name—"ababley"—in a slow, quavering scrawl. He was supposed to provide a second signature, but instead he wrote "signed by my hand hand" on a line that said: "date." Then he returned to the top line and added "hand" after "ababley." We removed the paper. Someone at the hospital accepted it, and we never heard of it again.

At home things were growing difficult. The very idea of home had become a concern for him. He was about to lose his life; he did not want to lose his bearings. Walking from the kitchen to the bedroom he asked my mother, "When am I going home?" His walking, once so vigorous, had become an elderly shuffle. When I told him about some minor setback of my own, he said with immense concern, "That's a disastrophe."

My mother was sleeping poorly and felt on the verge of collapse. A week after his final service, an ambulance took my father to the Queen Elizabeth Hospital, a mile from his apartment. The hospital would be closed down within a few years. We didn't realize that its small palliative-care unit was one of dubious quality.

It was lunchtime. My mother stayed for a few hours and then left to get some rest. As afternoon turned into evening and evening moved towards night, my father wandered the sixth floor, stepping into other people's rooms, having no idea where he was or what he was doing. I arrived at 9 p.m. and managed to settle him down, having been subjected to a well-justified complaint from another patient. It took an hour to get my father to bed. It was a hard struggle—I nearly had to push him down—but as soon as his head hit the sheets, he fell asleep, at a weird thirty-degree angle.

Home was now a pink-walled room looking west. I pinned a drawing by Kate on the bulletin board near a couple of get-well cards. Getting well was not an option. My mother brought a pot of azaleas.

I found myself wondering how old my father felt inside. Annie told me she had seen some document that he'd gone over at home; he signed it "Bunny Boy." He had become very fond of holding hands. On a weekend morning his palliative-care doctor, a woman in her thirties, appeared in his room, casually dressed, and he took her hand in his. A couple of minutes later I suggested he let go, and he replied, "I always hold the hand of beautiful ladies." The doctor laughed and said, "Naughty boy!"

In the face of loss and disintegration, small triumphs matter. After a few days in hospital my father's appetite returned, and his eyes lost the watery, blue-green filminess that had slipped over them. For a time, his mind cleared too. What made a difference was the replacement of morphine pills by a small patch on his skin. It released slow, continual hits of Fentanyl, a more potent drug than morphine. Fentanyl had not yet become a scourge on the street, where its many nicknames include jackpot, Apache, China girl, TNT, and, simply, friend. With the painkiller at a steady level in my father's bloodstream, lucidity came back to him.

So did hope. Ever eager for his compositions to be played and heard, he asked me to mail some of his chant settings to the editors of a collection being prepared in England. Having spent years as a freelance writer, I understood the impulse—the need for recognition, however late or small.

I stopped by my parents' apartment one morning, picked up the chant book and drove to the hospital. Then I spent an hour by my father's bedside, going through the book. It proved to be his musical life in miniature. All the hymn tunes and psalm chants he had composed and adapted over the decades were there, many in his own hand, some in my mother's. One was entitled "Coventry," another "Saskatoon." Among the terse melodies, for no apparent reason, was an article he had clipped from the *Guardian* about children in the Middle East who now carry guns.

We came across a simple chant and he stopped me from turning the page.

"I played this one at Heyope," he said. A tiny church in a Welsh hamlet not far from Knighton: his first appointment as an organist.

"And when was that?"

"I can't remember if it was before or after Mum died."

So he would have been fourteen or fifteen at the time, already composing music, turning scribbled notations into sounds that filled the air. Had I ever heard him use the word "Mum" to mean his own? Generally he used it to mean mine.

He selected a few chants that I promised to send off to England. But already his mood was darkening. Something, perhaps a jolt of pain, had forced him back to the present. He recalled where he was. He recalled why he was there.

"It's terrible," he said, "that I won't be playing at the church anymore. No services, no practices, no recitals…"

The idea made him desperate. I could offer no comfort.

38 In the middle of November my father left the palliative-care unit for a final spell at home. My mother, worn down by the demands of full-time caregiving in October, had needed a respite; now, she insisted, she was ready to cope. My father slowly changed out of his hospital gown and I drove him back to the low-rise apartment building where he had lived since the Barnsley fiasco. My parents rented a two-bedroom unit overlooking a leafy street. One of the bedrooms was given over to my father's work: thousands of musical scores; dozens of reel-to-reel tapes, and a machine that could still play them; concert programs, scrapbooks, music magazines; a postcard from the Beethoven House in Bonn, showing the opening bars of the "Moonlight Sonata"; photographs of churches and organs, a portrait of Bach. He walked into the apartment—the nine stairs leading up to it were a major effort—and sat down. Soon he fell asleep.

Amid all the proofs and icons of his past, he was at home. He could shuffle into the living room, rest on the couch, and feel that this, not some impersonal hospital room, was where he belonged. In previous years he had launched withering, despairing attacks on Montreal, attacks that often reached a punchline: "I don't want to die in this place!" Now that the process was underway, his urge to be elsewhere dissolved.

Some days he would sleep for seventeen or eighteen hours. When he woke up, he would be disoriented. What voices or tunes had he heard in his sleep? My father used to claim that he never dreamed; now his dreams were merging with the little that remained of waking life. One day he asked me if his voice sounded all right. I assured him that it did. "A few days ago," he said, "it was getting lost at the top of my head."

The sea of cancer, the tides of pain kept washing away the landmarks on his mental shore. One of the last to go was the urge to put things in order. He decided to phone the secretary of the Church of the Advent—though he got her name a little wrong—to explain that he was ill at the moment, wouldn't be able to come down to the church right now, but hoped to do so later…My mother gently reminded him of the x-rays that showed how far his malignancy had spread. Calmly, without rancour, he said, "Let's not talk about that now."

He made a tremendous effort when Annie and I brought our children over to see him one last time. At seven, Kate was old enough to sense the gravity of the event. She gave him enormous hugs at the start and end of the visit. She even gave his face a lick. He licked hers in return.

Sometimes he would ask to know the time. "It's 3 p.m.," I'd say, and he'd widen his eyes and pull back his head, as though in disbelief. The gesture was new to me. Nor could I recall his eyes being their present colour. His right eye had a pale, grey-blue tone. The left eye remained a little darker, a little greener. But his face hadn't collapsed the way I feared it would.

Strange fear. It would have made no difference to my father how he looked—he was beyond that kind of vanity, although he still cared about his dignity. My fear, I suppose, was that if his appearance altered in too dramatic a way, I would be unable to react to him normally. Yet what does "normal" mean when a father is about to die?

For me the blessing of his long, slow death was that it allowed me to rise a little way beyond the psychological entanglements of the past. To step beyond the mixture of love and frustration, tenderness and rage, that I had felt for nearly forty years, ever since I looked up from my playpen and saw him emerging naked from the bathroom. If his pain had any small reward, this was it. I was able, at last, to hold his hands, kiss his head, listen to his voice without anxiety. To be an open-hearted son. To react to his illness like a man.

I was able to love him without reserve. But what I struggle to admit is the knowledge that this love depended on his dying. A miraculous recovery on his part would have brought back all the tormented, jangled feelings on mine. Only in his last weeks could I finally say the simple words, "Dad, I love you."

39   It's possible, I guess, that much of what I've
      been lamenting in this book is nothing more
      than my father's bloody-mindedness. Perhaps
I was so quick to absorb my mother's tension that I over-
estimated the extent to which he was liable to say something hurtful to others or do something hurtful to himself.
My mother saw herself as a Canadian and, although her
political beliefs were on the left, she maintained the social
decorum of her friends in the Anglican Church. My father,
at heart, remained British. And a powerful strain in the
British character has always resisted what North Americans
might consider normality.

I think of a quote I found on the cover of Eric Newby's
memoir *Something Wholesale*, published in 1962: "The hero
of this book is not the author but Newby père. The head
of Lane & Newby is shown as a man after all our hearts,
a superb eccentric living, like the late Sir George Sitwell,
in a world that had altogether passed him by." Those lines

suggest that to become "a man after all our hearts," you would have to be both highly eccentric and determined to inhabit the past. Sir George was the inventor of a musical toothbrush and a miniature pistol for killing wasps. He put up a sign in his ancestral estate saying, "I must ask anyone entering the house never to contradict me in any way, as it interferes with the functioning of the gastric juices and prevents my sleeping at night." My father was not so flashily eccentric as that. But like Sir George, he refused to alter his actions or censor his words to suit other people's social conventions. He would go for long and solitary walks along the riverbanks of Saskatoon, declining the company of others. "If they don't like it," he said, "they can lump it."

The way I looked on him was not how other people saw him—that goes without saying. But did his colleagues and acquaintances have a clearer view of him than I did? Could I have seen him, all my life, through a glass darkly? He may have been one of those people who give the best of themselves to others and save the worst for the privacy of home. My father was a superb accompanist, adept at shaping the tones of an organ or piano to the needs of soloists and choirs. As an accompanist, as a conductor, as a teacher, he was neither eccentric nor bloody-minded. Going out into the world, he put on a brave face.

Or perhaps he didn't need to. Perhaps a brave face was what he required for life at home.

His unhappiness in Montreal, I now see, was related to his lack of students. In Saskatoon and Lethbridge, many of his pupils admired him—a few of them, I suspect, even loved him. He kept a framed photograph of a young ballerina near his bedside in Montreal; she had been one of his students, the recipient of his piano piece "Chelsea Reach." When my parents left Saskatoon, the girl's mother wrote a heartfelt letter: "Harry, as a teacher you have a unique and caring approach to your work and your students. I adore you as a teacher and a person and I know my children feel the same. Thank you for understanding Chelsea and allowing her to develop in her own way. Not everyone would have the patience to put up with her, but I think you tapped into her soul and saw the essence of her creativity. You allowed her to be a free spirit."

My father cared deeply for that family. Leaving them behind in Saskatoon must have been hard. I assumed that Annie and I could be a replacement for everything he'd given up, although I never bothered to think too much about what he had relinquished. And once my parents arrived in Montreal, I needed to keep them at arm's length. I didn't give a damn about Swindon Town, nor did I want to endure any more political rants. Above all, I was resolved to avoid either of my parents tapping into my soul or getting anywhere near the essence of my creativity.

What did my father want in the end? He had no interest in wealth. He never desired a big car or an expensive wardrobe. But he needed to feel useful, and he yearned to be recognized. "He's a human being," Willy Loman's wife tells her son in Arthur Miller's *Death of a Salesman*, "and a terrible thing is happening to him. So attention must be paid. He's not to be allowed to fall into his grave like an old dog. Attention, attention must be finally paid to such a person." The son resists his mother's plea. He is determined not to become like his father.

My father gave generously of his time, his energy, his talent. In Saskatoon, in Germany, attention was indeed paid. At other times and places he felt badly neglected. I rarely saw what he gave, but I grew intimate with his feeling of neglect.

40 He sat up in his bed one day in late November and I saw his neck: skin and bones. I had never understood that phrase before. All the muscle and fat, the sheer flesh, seemed to have gone. Gone where? My father's skin hung down in flaps from the jutting bones. His days and his body were shrinking in tandem.

One day he had a request for me. Two requests, in fact. My mother had gone off to the kitchen: for the moment we were alone together.

"When I'm gone," he said, "will you look after Mum?"

I nodded.

"And don't throw out my music, will you?"

He asked this almost shyly, as though fearful of my response.

"Of course I won't."

Little did I know how many thousands of pieces of paper I had just promised to preserve.

Another day I had an argument with my mother in the kitchen. My father was sitting in the living room, talking to his physician. She had brought along a student doctor, a young Chinese Canadian doing a residency in palliative care. The student's presence annoyed me: it emphasized that no matter how tremendous an event this was in the life of my family, it was a routine case in the wheels of the medical system. I was also, irrationally, annoyed because the doctors didn't know that ten minutes before they arrived, my father had been retching in the bathroom. Almost nothing came up except saliva. I held his forehead. He was remarkably stoic, remarkably grateful. Instead of mentioning this to the doctors, he assured them that he was "getting along all right, thanks." I wanted them to know this was untrue, but I also didn't want to contradict him. My mother bore the brunt of my stupid, helpless rage.

The young resident examined my father in the bedroom. When he made his way back into the living room, he was shivering uncontrollably. But he said nothing. He had become so thin that the shivering could not be avoided, still less cured.

Some confusion arose. "Harry," his doctor asked, "why couldn't you eat your breakfast this morning?"

"Oh, it was the strangest thing—the fried egg on the floor."

He smiled, not expecting us to understand, and we didn't. Breakfast had been a small bowl of cream of wheat, without an egg in sight. To break the awkward silence I walked over to the tape deck and put on a cassette entitled *Celtic Christmas*—gentle, melodic, tinged by a New Age atmosphere, almost seasonal now in late November.

My father jumped up. Everyone else stopped talking and looked at him. He ran to the piano—*ran!*—and, agitated, began to play a pair of notes with a finger, back and forth, back and forth. I turned off the cassette. My father sat down again. The rest of us behaved as if nothing had happened.

The doctors left. I left. When I phoned that evening, I asked my mother if she knew what had been going on. All he would say, she reported, was that a musical phrase "had got stuck in my head."

The next day she put on a tape of organ music. My father liked it, he admired the performance, but he had no idea that he was listening to himself. He told her it was a recording of Glenn Gould, playing the organ at Our Lady of Sorrows in Toronto.

41   I wrote my first poem in November 1961, at the age of six. We were living in Coventry at the time, renting the ground floor of a big house that had been subdivided into flats. That summer I had spent weeks in bed with whooping cough, enduring the boredom of wakeful hours staring at a pair of French windows with long, dark curtains. The garden beyond was an inaccessible stripe of green. Cats came and went. In the evening a blackbird sang.

When I was feeling better my father and his friend Peter took me to a football game: we stood on the terraces to watch Coventry City in blue play Swindon Town in red. (Swindon lost.) Back in Earlsdon Infants School I read chunks of *Winnie the Pooh* aloud to the class. At play time, tall boys gave out milk in glass bottles; the tall boys were seven years old. A bonfire on Guy Fawkes Night sent flames leaping into the sky above War Memorial Park. A week later, looking ahead to Christmas, I took pencil to paper:

The Great Lover
Loves us all,
Go to the manger,
He is there.

The King of all,
The Master of all,
The Lover of all,
Is God of all.

Go and see Him
With presents in your hands,
Go and love Him,
King of all.

My father typed these words on a small sheet of heavy paper with a two-barred cross at the top and an arch of holly below. When I turn the sheet over now, I find a reproduction of Canada's Christmas Seals from our time in Sault Ste. Marie. He must have saved the blank page, waiting for a rainy day or a lyrical son. For years he preserved a wartime mentality: never throw anything out that might be useful in the future. Shortly after I wrote those lines, we caught a bus to Liverpool, a passenger ship to Montreal, and a long, slow train across the continent to southern Alberta.

I have absolutely no memory of producing the poem. What I remember, with acute embarrassment, is that years later my father turned it into an anthem for choir and organ. "Words by Mark Abley: Music by Henry Abley," the score reads at the top. My father added the precise date: "12th Nov. 1961." He set the poem to music in D major—"the key of glory," as it was known in the Baroque period—and, at the top, wrote "Flowingly." The musical notes on the page are in his hand but the words between the bars are written in my mother's tidy script. A family project; a team effort. My father made the second stanza a kind of refrain, bringing it back at the end.

My acute embarrassment arose because he persuaded a soloist to sing this anthem at First Baptist Church when I was eleven, and inveigled the choir at St. John's Cathedral to sing it when I was in university. By then I was writing poetry of a more, let's say, sophisticated nature, and the possibility that anyone might see these lines as representative of my mature *oeuvre* was enough to mortify me. (As a teenager I was easily mortified.) Listening to the choir sing my childish words, I stared straight ahead, my face a mask, refusing to acknowledge the smiles in the congregation. I have succeeded in forgetting what the music sounded like. As far as I know, it has never been heard since.

Flash forward to the autumn of 1981, when several of my father's compositions were performed at the launch of

Canada Music Week in Saskatoon. Dozens of musicians, hundreds in the audience at Third Avenue United—it must have been a great event. The indefatigable Eric Burt wrote an article to promote the concert, and looking at the yellowed clipping now I'm startled by two brief paragraphs in the middle:

> One item of particular interest will be Abley's musical setting of the John Freeman poem Music Comes. This was written during the past summer as a wedding gift for the Ableys' son, Mark, and his bride, who were married in England.
>
> The song was not sung at the wedding and will have its first public performance when it is sung by Helen Pridmore on this occasion.

My father played the organ at my wedding; indeed he performed one of his compositions for the instrument while Annie and I signed the register in a corner of the stone church. This proved to be a deafening task, as the register stood on a table beneath the organ pipes. Our first act as a married couple was to shout at each other over my father's music.

He had given us a copy of "Music Comes" a few days earlier. I hope I managed to express a little gratitude, but the poem's plodding rhythms, treacly images, and predictable rhymes annoyed me. It had been published in 1921, just before modernist work like *The Waste Land* swept such odes away. I stuck the score in a cupboard and forgot all about it. But reading the *Star-Phoenix* article now, I wonder if my father felt aggrieved that Annie and I had not plucked a soprano out of thin air. "The song was not sung…"

Five years later, my father asked me to introduce the music at a recital in the Church of the Advent. He'd been living in Montreal for a year by then, and already it was clear that, musically speaking, the experience was a debacle. As an organist his glory days, if that's the right phrase, were in the past: for many works in his repertoire, the small organ at his disposal was simply inadequate. I was surprised by his request—previous recitals had needed no introductions—but I agreed to it. One way or another, I always seemed to be looking for ways to cheer him up. I drove over to my parents' apartment, light snow falling on the icy streets, and asked about the works on the program. It felt strange to take notes as if I were interviewing my father for a newspaper article, but soon I had all the material I needed.

Then, on a Sunday afternoon in early December, I stood up, walked to the front of the church, and began to speak: " 'Legend' was written by my father earlier this year in memory of the former premier of Saskatchewan and leader of the New Democratic Party, Tommy Douglas.

My father is performing it today by special request. 'Legend' is based on two medieval plainsong themes, which will be played at the beginning of the work. These themes appear separately, and later recur simultaneously and in chorale form. Towards the end, the music rises to a kind of affirmation…"

And so on. The special request was my mother's.

"Legend" wasn't the only obscure piece on the program; a couple of the other composers also needed introducing. It was not a standard program, but the list of pieces didn't worry me; what concerned me was the number of people who would be there to hear my father play. Twenty? Fifteen? Ten? Montreal is full of things to do on a Sunday afternoon before Christmas. Entering a small church in Westmount to hear organ music by Henry Abley, Alberto Ginastera, and Léon Boëllmann is high on nobody's agenda.

I sat beside my mother, clenched upright in her usual pew near the front. Before the recital began, she turned around every couple of minutes to see if anyone else had come through the heavy wooden door. Inside her hand-knitted cardigan, her shoulders were taut with tension. Whether the audience was small or large, I was confident my father would play the music well—he was a professional, and professionals do their job without complaint. I had learned that from him, and would try to remember it whenever the attendance at a poetry reading was lower than twenty, or fifteen, or ten. But if the audience was minuscule I knew my mother would pay a heavy price. My father's morale would be impaired for weeks. A sense of futility would corrode his spirits. His bilious attacks on Montreal would become ever more acid.

That day, the light fading over the city, the church not quite warm enough for comfort, there were just enough bodies in the pews for my father to feel it had not all been a waste of time. I was relieved. I had spoken my piece; I had done my duty.

But I was taken aback when my father followed up by asking me if we could put on an event together. A joint recital, he suggested: my poetry, his pieces for organ. A double act, father and son.

Embarrassment surged back. Poetry readings take place in cafés and bars, libraries and bookstores. Those venues do not contain pipe organs. My poems were not religious—could I read them, with a straight face, in a church? That's the excuse I made to myself. But the truth was this: in my early thirties, trying to make my way as a writer in Montreal, I didn't want my poems to be connected with unfashionable music performed by an old man on an old, unfashionable instrument. Many of my friends were Jews, atheists, or both; would any of them show up for an event inside a church? There seemed to be something forced, something ridiculous, about the whole idea. I was stubborn. He had his pride; I had my pride too.

Now I wish I'd had the audacity to say yes. It would have been a brave experiment—and isn't that what art is all about? In suggesting this double act, my father was more original, less bound by convention than I was. He was the true artist; I was still a young pretender, and I didn't even realize it. Nor did I see that by extending the offer, my father was showing me how much he respected my own vocation.

I should have been honest enough to say no. But I never gave my father a straight answer. I let his invitation fade into the long silence between us.

I'm sure I disappointed him in this. By then I was old enough to realize that my father had taught me a lot: about the need to practise a craft and perfect a technique, about the commitment an artist's life requires, and about perseverance in the face of rejection. But I had learned something else too: the power of silence.

42 An ambulance came back for him one morning at the beginning of December. Stretcher-bearers carried him down the nine steps, through the front lobby and out to the waiting vehicle. The cold air must have stung when they swung the doors wide open, for my father was wearing only a dressing gown, pyjamas, and slippers. These were his final breaths of open air.

He returned to the sixth floor of the hospital because my mother, riddled with fatigue, couldn't cope any longer. It seemed an admission of failure, one that bothered her later. But he kept getting up in the night, and she had difficulty coaxing him back to bed. We didn't have the money to pay for weeks of private nursing. A friend gently pointed out to my mother that she'd been doing all the cooking, serving, cleaning, and nursing—jobs performed by many people in a hospital. Annie and I hadn't offered much practical help either. We had full-time jobs, two young children, and a home of our own to think about. But this absence, this withdrawal on my part, would trouble me in the months to come.

Now his hospital room had pale blue walls adorned by a calendar of Claude Monet's garden and a laminated photograph in a thin metal frame. With his pillows raised, my father looked towards the Canadian Shield in early spring: a mass of white trilliums in the foreground, spindly trees in the middle distance, and a dark, two-storey wooden house. Beyond, the world receded into a backdrop of darkness and confusion.

With my father installed and asleep, I went off to verify that his arrival had been registered. I came back to his room a few minutes later and found him wide awake. We shuffled up and down the corridor, arm in arm. He noticed an amateur painting near the nursing station: a child with a lamb.

"I remember that chicken!" he said.

His mind could still sort ideas into the right general categories: animals on a farm; meat for a Welsh butcher. But within each category, he could no longer be sure of locating the proper item. Mental borders were slackening. Words were spilling over the edges. "They think I'm going out of my mad," he said one day.

After I left the hospital, driving back along the highway to a treed suburb where the houses already sported Christmas lights, my father rose in the night, agitated, wandering. Somehow his colostomy bag came off. A nurse found him, reconnected him, and put him into bed with a sedative. The next morning he was confused, saying this had happened two nights ago, and insisting, "I put myself back together and got back to bed." He knew he was no longer whole. Yet the hunger to be capable had won out, in his mind, over the bleak fact of helplessness.

His weakness embarrassed him. Asking a nurse for a cup of fruit juice, he added: "I'm so soft!" This was not, I suppose he felt, how a man was supposed to act. To make the room feel less impersonal, more a semblance of home, my mother taped up a drawing by Kate, showing a smiling sun, two horses, and a little pony. In the sky, Kate had written: "I love my granny and grandad."

One afternoon I arrived at the hospital to find him in a light haze of sleep. I gave him a couple of ice chips to moisten his mouth—the ancient, primordial urge to help had come down to its most basic level. When my mother entered the room, he beckoned to her with his lips, and she kissed him. He sipped a little Ensure, the vitamin-packed drink that was, by now, sustaining him. My mother held the glass, her hand trembling.

I watched him in his sleep, or near-sleep. A Baroque concerto grosso was playing on the tape deck, and his left hand stretched out over the bed cover. Purple veins jutted out from the papery skin. His fingers moved a few times, as though to conduct the music.

Later he woke again. The first sign was a strange shivering of his lower lip and chin. The shivering lasted a few seconds, stopped, began again, stopped again. Finally his eyes opened. But they stared at me as though unseeing.

"Mum's here," I said.

"Where's Mum?" he answered. He clambered out of bed, desperate to reach the toilet. I helped him there and tried to rub his back when he had finished. "Let me go!" he said through clenched teeth. A nurse appeared and led him in a macabre, face-to-face dance to the bed. He shuffled there with great concentration, the nurse taking small steps backward, my father moving slowly forward. When he rolled into bed, he began to shiver uncontrollably. My mother and I pulled up both blankets. He was still shivering when I left.

I returned in the morning to find his bed a mass of urine. It had been many hours since he was changed.

After he was cleaned up and wearing dry pyjamas, I persuaded him to drink a little Ensure through a straw. He complied. But after the first sip he looked at me and said, "It won't make any difference, will it?"

To stop him falling or wandering, the nurses fastened a harness-like restraint over his bed at night. He was a prisoner now, not just of his dying body but of the entire medical system. "This is not what palliative care should be like," I thought to myself. But I didn't complain. My father was

British and dying, and the British—his kind, anyway—are loath to make a fuss.

Outside, the ground lay bare. Dead leaves tossed in the wind. A sign on the hospital wall announced, "The Siamese connections supply the sprinkler system." What the hell does that mean? I asked myself. What the hell does anything mean?

43 When I was a boy, my father would occasionally be asked to serve as an adjudicator for music festivals elsewhere in Saskatchewan. He was happy to do this—it meant a bit of travel, some extra money, a chance to do something different. Restlessness was part of what defined him. One year an invitation arrived from a festival in Swift Current, a three-hour drive away from Saskatoon. I can't recall if the event took place in late fall or early spring. Whenever it was, a massive blizzard hit the province, choking the highways, making road travel next to impossible.

My father set out anyway. There were no cellphones or emails in those days, and nobody from Swift Current phoned our house in the early morning. The Beetle had no tire chains, heated wiper blades, or any of the other accessories that soften the impact of blizzards for drivers today; it was a small car inching along two-lane roads through high winds and blowing snow. More than six hours after his car backed out of the driveway, my father arrived in

Swift Current. The festival organizers couldn't believe it—given the extreme weather, they assumed he would have stayed home. "You have true English grit," one of them said, a compliment my father enjoyed.

In an unassuming way, he was physically brave. He once stepped into the office of Third Avenue United, in Saskatoon's downtown core, to find the secretary being harassed by a tall and heavy man. It was morning, but the man had been drinking. He wanted money.

My father decided to put a stop to this. But instead of phoning for help or hurrying to the nearby police station, he confronted the intruder. He told the man to leave the church at once. He didn't stop to consider if this was the wisest move for a small man of sixty-five who needed to take care of his hands.

The intruder turned around and swung a fist into my father's face. He dropped to the floor with a broken nose. So much for gallantry.

The man was Cree. Yet this incident had no effect on my father's respect for Indigenous people. He'd already composed a musical setting for the Anglican liturgy that he dedicated to St. Kateri Tekakwitha of the Mohawks. He would go on to adapt the "Huron Carol" and to write "The Pines of Oka." Indians, in his mind, were exploited by governments and big corporations. They had little or no power. He was on their side.

He didn't complain about the way his broken nose left him with a slightly unsymmetrical face. He hadn't complained about the slipped discs and gallbladder pains of middle age. Nor would he complain about chemotherapy, radiation, invasive surgery, and a colostomy bag. He complained instead about the decline of music, the decline of railways, the decline of socialism, the decline of Swindon Town, the decline of churches, the decline of quality television—every perceived decline except his own. It's a good thing he didn't live to see the replacement of pipe organs by digital technology, a decline that would have thrown all his other complaints in the shade.

Even when depression held him in its grip, he didn't want to admit it. As Kierkegaard once wrote, "The specific character of despair is precisely this: it is unconscious of being despair." That rings uncomfortably true for my father's life in Montreal. Yet as long as he could find grounds for hope—a new piece of music, an upcoming recital, a move to a different city—was he ever in complete despair? I prefer to believe that he always had bursts of hope, and the hope nourished him. People could disappoint him. They often did. But music would not fail.

My father never accused Bach of letting him down. Solo Dei Gloria.

44 "Damned good show....Your music hath charms....Here's to the next time": praise scrawled on the program of "Victory Variety" on a May evening in 1945. A cassette of an organ recital broadcast across Canada on a Sunday afternoon. A taste for civilized British mysteries and the detectives who untangle them: Brother Cadfael, Inspector Morse. A shaving brush, razor blades, a jar of shaving cream. A portable typewriter, a monogrammed handkerchief. Good times. Colostomy supplies. A prayer to St. Jude, the patron of lost causes, clipped from a newspaper and stashed in a leather wallet near a *Peanuts* cartoon. A dream of Our Lady of Sorrows. Ashes under rose bushes pouring their scent across a Wiltshire churchyard.

What does a life add up to?

Smiles in photograph albums that his grandchildren may unearth, one day, curious to see what their father's father looked like. A box of slides recalling summer days with his wife and child at English Bay, Lost Lagoon, Siwash Rock. His memory, receding day by day, in the minds of ministers he worked with, students he taught, fellow organists who appreciated his incisive touch with Messiaen, his cool gravity with Bach. A fondness for leg of lamb and mint sauce, roast potatoes and peas. Wind streaming from the west across a heather-covered hill. The feel of that wind on his young face. Good times. The feel of a catheter, needles, an iv. Musical scores he wrestled over, a pencil behind an ear, scores unopened since his death. Scores that will never be performed again. His slim fingers poised on the manuals of a great organ in a German church, a cinema organ in London, a mulish organ in Saskatoon, a little organ in Montreal, a pump organ in a Welsh hamlet.

What does a life add up to?

A Saskatchewan licence plate in a Montreal study. Shoes he never wore except to play the organ. Stray copies of letters that survived the countless moves across a city, a country, an ocean. The formal: "No doubt you will let me know if you wish to pursue my application, or if you have already made an appointment, as I can see may well be the case." The informal: "Weather is very hot and oppressive—too much thunder about! We've had some pretty nifty storms, and it looks like another cooking up now." Pencilled notes in a Masonic handbook, *The Ancient Working of Trinity*

Lodge, Coventry, No. 254: "Improv," "Charity," "Reception," "For every stormy wind," "That duty is performed," "PLAY A PIECE." A review stiffly translated from a Geneva newspaper and quoted in his concert brochure: "The dominant quality of the playing of Henry Abley is a stability which provides his musical intentions with an exemplary clarity." Good times. Damned good show, if anyone was there to hear it.

What does a life add up to?

An airline ticket to romantic places; a broken nose. A cigarette that bears a lipstick's traces; a touch on a son's hand. A lick on a grandchild's cheek. The scent of pipe tobacco. A clutch of names: Harry Knight, Pte. H.T. Abley 173646, Bunny Hunch, Henry T. Abley, Nubbo, ababley. Anger, prejudice, resentment, doubt, migraines—all gone now, over and done with, vanished. Generosity, kindness, loyalty, exemplary clarity—also vanished. The care with which he battled to comb strands of hair over an ever-growing bald patch. A widow: her memories of touch. Good times. The filmy surface of his eyes as death drew near. These fragments I have shored against my ruin. A son: also moody, also self-absorbed, also bad at dancing; a look in my eyes, the cast of my mouth, the same as his. A son whose slim fingers also interpret the world on a keyboard, crying out to a silent room, "What am I doing?"

I ask you.

45 The snow arrived to stay one morning in the second week of December, first a minor sprinkling, then a major fall. I talked to my mother that evening, and the news was bad. My father had been clutching his crotch, and when he drank some Ensure, he told her, "Now I'll pay for it." Another time he said to her, "This is embarrassing, you know there are ugly words for this, I don't like them." She said, "Yes, we don't use them, but you mean you have pain in your private parts." He said, "Oh yes."

In the night he fell again. A nurse discovered him on the floor of the bathroom, where he'd blindly made his way. God knows how long he'd been lying there. He had struggled out of the cloth harness and clambered over the bed's metal rails. By then his Fentanyl patch had been increased to 50 milligrams, and my mother saw with dismay that a doctor had ordered a renewal until the end of February. Two and a half more months of this?

Annie and I went out to a restaurant one night, then a Christmas party. It felt both heartless and necessary. The next morning I told Megan, now a year and three-quarters old, "Vicky put you to bed." She repeated: "Vicky put to bed." It was the first time I'd heard her use a preposition. I hated myself for noticing this.

In the afternoon we took the children to the *Gazette* Christmas party, where some of the staffers were strolling around in costume. Megan remembered the scene at bedtime, saying with a smile as she looked over my shoulder: "Santa Claus…Mickey Mouse…Goofy!" She was moving beyond infancy just as my father was regressing into it. He could no longer bathe or feed himself. His words were getting mixed up. His sleep patterns were irregular. His food was semi-solid or liquid. He had to wear a diaper.

One day I noticed that his mouth looked dry. "Are you thirsty, Dad?" I said. "Would you like an ice chip in your mouth?"

"Would you?" he replied.

"I will if you will."

"All right then."

So I walked past the artificial tree in the corridor to an ice machine by the elevators. In a minute I was back with a Styrofoam cup full of ice chips, but my father had fallen asleep.

When he was awake, he seemed to enjoy hearing a cassette of Schubert's pieces for piano. Music for organ or choir, however, distressed him. "I just want to go home," he kept saying. "When can I go home?"

And sometimes: "What do I have to do next?"

He knew what he had to do next.

What I had to do was drive to a seniors' residence and report on its elaborate Christmas pageant. As a feature writer, I'd been writing background articles for the newspaper about large and terrible subjects: the Holocaust, the Armenian genocide, human rights abuses in Asia. It was a relief to be asked to cover something less demanding. "I'm off now," I told him, "but Mum will be coming in soon."

"Which Mum?" he said.

I watched the pageant from the back of the hall. One of the three kings suffered from Alzheimer's. The Virgin Mary was almost blind. After the curtain opened and Joseph kissed her mottled cheek, she wandered offstage. The director strode halfway up the aisle and said in a loud voice, "Go back, Mary—the angel wants to talk to you." The angel wore a gold halo and a lace tablecloth.

Annie came to the hospital one day when my mother was present. My father held Annie's hand and stroked it. "It feels warm and cold," he said, "like a woman I knew in the war." My mother's face was thunder.

Father Warren arrived in jeans and an old blue sweater, bringing my father communion in the form of a previously consecrated wafer. I closed the door of the room and put a "Do Not Disturb" sign on it. The service was radically shortened. My father stayed awake throughout and seemed glad that his priest had come. He managed to swallow the wafer.

By now he had two patches of Fentanyl, but one evening in mid-December he was again in terrible pain. A nurse brought him an extra pill and grew annoyed when he couldn't slide it down his throat. "Concentrate!" she barked.

I found it hard to get used to the idea that soon, all this would be a memory; that the memories could never be added to; that over the years, they would only diminish. As my father lay dying, I found myself consciously storing up the memories, adding to them almost obsessively in the certain knowledge that the subtraction would soon begin. *These foolish things remind me of...*

I went into the hospital one afternoon and found him asleep. He woke up and needed the toilet. That task accomplished, a nurse and I manoeuvred him into a chair.

"How are you?" I said.

"Not so bad. Getting on."

But his face was tighter, his colour more pallid.

He complained about his teeth. I tried to brush them but he couldn't remember how to rinse. Water dripped down onto his pyjama pants. My mother walked in at that point and grew upset. She tried to mop up the little spill, complaining that I didn't know how to do things. My father reached out with his left hand and pumped my arm a couple of times in support. Then he wanted to give my mother a kiss. And when I thought he was drifting off to sleep, he suddenly leaned forward and rubbed noses with me, back and forth.

The day before, my mother said, he'd been convinced there was a grey cat on the floor. For breakfast he ate cream of wheat, some yellow custard, a cup of clear tea, a glass of orange juice, a glass of Ensure, and half of a small carton of milk—everything that was on offer, as if he were stoking up for the final challenge. Now he was refusing food except for a few sips of soup.

My father woke up when I was there and Amanda, his favourite nurse, was leaning over him. He reached out almost blindly and ran his hand up Amanda's arm. It was a shockingly sexual gesture. I pulled his hand gently away.

46

"Are you ready?" my father said.

"I think so."

"Right then."

He took a breath and began to play the Fantasia and Fugue in C Minor, BWV 537, by J.S. Bach. If he was nervous, he didn't show it. We were together in the organ loft of a medieval church on a summer evening in 1980, and the instrument at his fingertips—one of the grand organs of northern Germany—had been installed when Bach was a child. My father was on a tour of Lower Saxony during which he would play five concerts in eight days; he and my mother would travel on to Berlin for further recitals before they flew home to Saskatoon. I was a young freelancer, based in London, attempting to live by words. Despite some trepidation—the image of a locked door in a small hotel was still etched in my mind—I had joined my parents for a week.

When I agreed to do this, I didn't know that my father would seek my help in two of his recitals. Not with the small, modern organs he would play on the East Frisian Islands, where families on holiday try to pretend that the North Sea is as alluring as the Mediterranean: in the churches there he could turn the pages and change the stops without help. But the big, historic organ of the Martinikirche in Bremen posed a challenge. So did the instrument I was facing now, high above the floor of the Ludgerikirche in the ancient port of Norden. It had been constructed in 1687 by Arp Schnitger, a celebrated organ builder who retained some of the pipes from the Ludgerikirche's previous organ, dating back to the mid-sixteenth century. The instrument has no pistons or combination stops, making the set-up for each piece a cumbersome, time-consuming process. Each individual stop is mounted on a dowel of wood stretching out several inches. Organists who have to pull some stops out and push others in during a piece are at risk of damaging the flow and rhythm of the music.

Hence the need for an assistant, though in the Ludgerikirche, luckily, the stops have numbers as well as names. My father would take care of the stops to his right; I would handle the ones to his left. The job was not exactly onerous. I was worried, even so, that I would commit a grievous blunder, making the trumpet blare forth in a quiet passage, or pulling out the flute a second too late. Having read little sheet music in the past few years, I was unsure of myself, and there had been time for only one rehearsal. Luckily the registration for the fantasia was simple. A sombre piece, it evokes a wealth of loss and sorrow.

Through most of the fantasia I could relax, leaning against a wall near a wooden angel. It was easy to imagine, caught up in the flowing music, that this organ was immune to the ailments of history. An illusion: in 1943 it had been dismantled and removed from Norden, a potential target for Allied bombs, to be stored for safety at a nearby monastery. A German soldier might have spirited the organ off in a truck on the same night that my father was driving a similar vehicle on a lightless road across the sea…The fantasia twined and curled to a graceful resolution, pulling me from my reverie. In the vibrant, bustling fugue, I had to add a stop called, confusingly, the "mixture."

My father moved on to a piece he loved, Bach's Fantasia in G Major, BWV 572. Its showpiece opening leads into a long and majestic central section, during which my father's feet moved easily on the pedals and his hands roamed the manuals' ivory keys, mellowed to a dusky orange colour with the sweat of centuries, as if this high and ancient organ loft were not a fragment of foreign territory but his natural home. I had three turns in the score to watch out for, and a stop to add just before the regal lines of the central movement gave way to an astonishing finale, rising arpeggios on a manual matched to a falling sequence in the pedals. Somehow the inner voices of the piece, all speaking rapidly at once, flow together to create an inevitable harmony. When performed well, the finale has a strangely weightless quality, the notes transcending gravity and floating on waves of air. My father performed it well.

Next came "Fugue, Chorale, and Epilogue" by the English composer Herbert Howells. It kept me busy. There were seventeen stops for us to pull out before the piece began, some to subtract as it went along, and others to add. After the Howells had drawn to a close, a work by Lotte Backes—somewhat overwrought, I felt, though I did not say this aloud—required a tricky pair of page turnings while my father's hands were unrelentingly busy. A brief eighteenth-century gavotte—it reminded me of a mouth-refreshing sorbet in the middle of a feast—preceded a big passacaglia and fugue by the Canadian composer Healey Willan, and for ease of sight-reading I was relieved that the main theme of the passacaglia remains in the pedals throughout. In addition to the printed score, I had a page of handwritten notes to follow. On page 5, my father needed me to pull out #5 and #11. On page 9, I had to get rid of #5, #11, and #13, and introduce #26. On the final page, with the music building to a crescendo, I had to add #20.

As he had done so often in the past, as he would do so often in the future, my father played an ethereal, shimmering piece by Olivier Messiaen. If the eternal church really looks anything like it sounds in his "Apparition de l'église éternelle," the devout are in for a treat. There, too, I had some stops to change in mid-piece. The recital finished with a complete change of mood and registration: a late Romantic work by a German composer named Sigfrid Karg-Elert, its main theme based on the melody of a Martin Luther hymn. In the triumphant final bars of "Ein feste Burg ist unser Gott," my father and I came close to pulling out all the stops.

A mighty fortress is our God. Then silence. Somewhere alone in the pews below sat my proud mother. My father swung his legs over the organ bench, stood up, moved into view of the audience, and took a bow. I didn't applaud, I just stood there grinning. Atop the organ loft in the Ludgerikirche, an angel from the Book of Revelation forever blows a slender trumpet. I felt as if this angel, the wooden angel beside me, and all the angels in the church were saluting my father's work.

Many years later, at the Banff Centre for the Arts, I mentioned this experience to a fellow writer. Andreas had just read from a novella, only part of it fictional, based on his own father. Theirs had been a tense relationship, never completely resolved. When I described travelling with my parents in northern Germany and changing the stops in the organ loft, he leaned across and slapped my knee. I was surprised: this was not a man I knew well.

His face was creased in a smile.

"You lucky bastard!" he said.

47 A small hospital in the west end of Montreal, set back a few streets from the highway.

"Let me off!" my father said. It was the last thing I heard him say, and he said it three times. It was a week before Christmas. The first time I replied, "It's OK, Dad, you're in the hospital."

"Let me off!"

My mother said, "Where do you want to be let off?"

"Let me off!"

The next morning, a nurse couldn't rouse him. He was breathing loudly, snoring often, and he would groan from time to time. The nurses had to move him occasionally to prevent bedsores. Each time they handled him, he groaned.

In the coma, his mouth stayed open, I could see far back into it: he seemed to have half-swallowed his tongue, it was so small and rolled and distant. But the nurses said this was typical. His eyes were not quite shut; the whites remained visible under the lids. Apparently this was typical too. To my mother, to me, nothing was typical.

That day I was shocked to see his legs, bare below the diaper. So little flesh was left. The hip bones protruded so obviously. One of them was bruised, and a nurse asked my mother if it had been broken. There were purple bruises lower down his legs too.

The nurses brought a cot into the room. My mother and I took turns lying on the cot and sitting on the chair beside his bed. We held his hands. I talked to him briefly: "Hi Dad. It's Mark. I love you." My mother's presence constrained me from saying more. I fear my presence constrained her too. His breathing was unpredictable, sometimes halting for a few seconds, then hurrying forward. In the night he had a strange short spell of whimpering, almost like a bird. We thought he must be dying then, but the whimpering stopped and his lungs carried on their work. By early morning he was breathing shallowly.

At 6:30 a.m. the night nurse gave him an extra dose of painkiller through a butterfly needle in his left arm, and rolled him over. He still had enough vitality to groan. The rolling seemed to revive him: his breathing grew stronger again.

By that time my mother's dentures were troubling her badly, and she wanted to change into fresh clothes. So she left the hospital and went back to her apartment for an hour.

I was alone with him then. Over the brick houses, their front doors wreathed with ersatz holly and ivy, sunlight had begun to break. December 20: one of the shortest days in the year. The frosty streets, the schools, even the office buildings shone with Christmas decorations. I put on a cassette of choral music from my father's days in Saskatoon. The singing voices bothered me, though, and after a few seconds I pressed Stop and removed the cassette. Was this a time for silence?

I hesitated, then chose another tape from a small pile on the bedside table, slid it into the machine, and pressed Play. A melody began to unfurl. After adjusting the volume I sat beside my father, reached below the blanket and took his hands. For most of the previous day they had lain by his side. The night nurse must have folded them on top of his chest.

Then I spoke to my father. I told him how brave he had been over the past couple of years, how much I admired his courage, and how in the patience with which he endured pain and indignity he had shown me some of what it means to be a man. I asked him not to be afraid: he would be going home now. I said his mother would be waiting to meet him.

I wished him luck on the next journey, the great voyage. And I told him again how much I had learned from him about the vocation of an artist.

I had no idea if my father could hear me. Yet almost immediately, something happened. His eyes changed.

Instead of remaining slightly open, they shut completely. His head jerked forward a little on the pillow. He took three or four small breaths—then nothing. It was as if his spirit had decided to leave. I watched the pulse along the side of his neck. It stopped. I couldn't believe it: the simplicity, the peacefulness. I thought, "Has he really died?"

As if in answer, long seconds after the previous breath, he gave another one: a short exhalation.

I watched and waited: no more pulse, no more breath. No more pain, no more indignity. Sitting by the bed, I kept holding his hands and looking at his face. No more good times. No more other times. There was still some warmth in his hands. I heard a door open as if from far away. In the clean light of a winter morning a nurse came in and found us there, the blue-walled room echoing with organ music: Johann Sebastian Bach's Fantasia and Fugue in C Minor, BWV 537, being played by my dead father.

ACKNOWLEDGEMENTS

This book has been a very long time in the making. Its first reader was my wife, Ann Beer. I am grateful beyond words for her love, her support, her astute criticisms, and her constant enthusiasm for the project. I also give thanks to my daughter Megan, another very early reader of the book, with much gratitude for her intelligent comments and many apologies for the tears she shed.

In particular I want to thank my son Kayden. He appears in these pages in his original identity. I felt it would have been a betrayal of the truth to pretend that my parents ever knew him as a grandson rather than a granddaughter, and I admire his courage, in this as in so many other ways, for allowing me to name and describe him as I've done in these pages.

If you've read the book, you'll understand how much I owe to Tom Murison and Tom Packham. I am very grateful to them both, and also to my old friends Martha Baillie, David Macfarlane, and Ronald Wright for their generosity in reading a version of the manuscript and offering an endorsement of it.

Outside my family, the book's first readers were my friends Derek Webster and Denis Sampson. Both of them made a number of shrewd and valuable suggestions for improvement. The book is much the better for their remarks. I thank T.F. Rigelhof, Kim Echlin, Scott Lawrence, and David Manicom, who read a complete early version; Eric Siblin for information about pipe organs and J.S. Bach; and Charles Foran, who told me, even before my father's death, that I needed to write a book about my relationship with the man.

A few of the chapters were drafted, many years ago, at the Banff Centre for the Arts. My thanks to Michael Ignatieff, who offered sage advice.

I'm grateful to my agent, Jackie Kaiser of Westwood Creative Artists, for commenting on the manuscript and working hard to sell the book, and to Bruce Walsh of the University of Regina Press for being willing to take a risk on it. Thanks also to Sean Prpick, Kelly Laycock, Duncan Campbell, and everyone else at the press, and especially to Ryan Perks for a superb job of copy-editing. Jason Safdie and Susan Lacoste transformed cassettes and reel-to-reel tapes of my father's recitals into digital files; my warmest thanks to them and to Elie Tordjman, who helped me put old photographs and soundtracks of my father onto my website, www.markabley.com.

A grant from the Canada Council for the Arts sustained me over a stretch of writing time. I thank the council for the grant and for all the work it does.

"Mother and Son" and "Cancer" were published in *The Tongues of Earth: New and Selected Poems* (Coteau Books, 2015). I want to thank the publisher, John Agnew, for allowing them to be reprinted here. "Parade" first appeared in *Global Poetry Anthology 2015* (Véhicule Press). Two other poems included in this book are printed here for the first time.

As for the complex and boundless debt I owe my father and mother, what more can I say?

ABOUT THE AUTHOR

Mark Abley has written six books of non-fiction, four collections of poetry, and two children's books. His *Spoken Here: Travels Among Threatened Languages* won international acclaim and has been widely translated. Abley is a Rhodes Scholar, a Guggenheim Fellow and a winner of Canada's National Newspaper Award, and he was the first Canadian recipient of the LiberPress Prize for international writers. His work has been published in *The Guardian* and *The Times*; he has spoken at both Oxford and Cambridge universities; and he contributes to the *Times Literary Supplement*. In 2018 Simon & Schuster Canada published his book *Watch Your Tongue: What Our Everyday Sayings and Idioms Figuratively Mean*.